HUMAN BODY EXPLORER

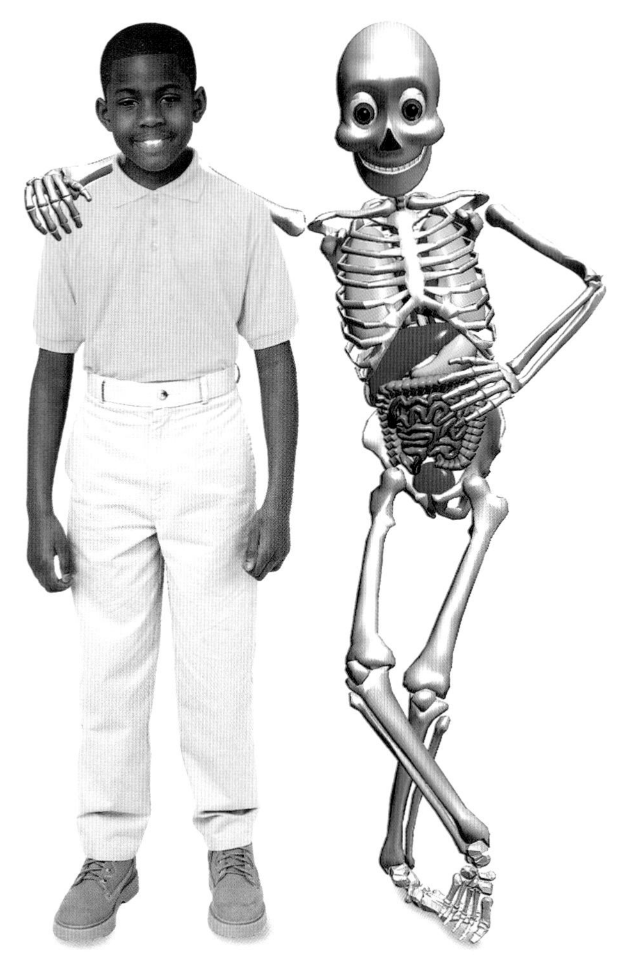

PAUL DAWSON

MEDICAL CONSULTANT
DR. PETE ROWAN

A Dorling Kindersley Book

LONDON, NEW YORK, SYDNEY, DELHI,
PARIS, MUNICH & JOHANNESBURG

Senior Editor Carey Scott
Senior Designer Chris Scollen
Senior DTP Designer Bridget Roseberry
Production Controller Erica Rosen

Managing Editor Linda Martin
Managing Art Editor Peter Bailey
US Editor Chuck Wills

Produced for Dorling Kindersley by

studio cactus 

13 SOUTHGATE STREET WINCHESTER HAMPSHIRE SO23 9DZ

Editor Jane Baldock
Designer Sharon Moore

Published in the United States by
Dorling Kindersley Publishing, Inc.
95 Madison Avenue
New York, New York 10016

First American Edition, 2000
00 01 02 03 04 05 10 9 8 7 6 5 4 3 2 1

Dorling Kindersley books are available at special discounts for bulk purchases for sales promotions or premiums. Special editions, including personalized covers, excerpts of existing guides, and corporate imprints can be created in large quantities for specific needs. For more information, contact Special Markets Dept./Dorling Kindersley Publishing, Inc./ 95 Madison Ave./New York, NY 10016/Fax: 800-600-9098.

Library of Congress Cataloging-in-Publication Data

Dawson, Paul Robert, 1962-
Human body explorer / by Paul Dawson.-- 1st American ed.
p. cm.
"First published in Great Britain in 2000 by Dorling Kindersley Limited."
Includes index.
Summary: Describes the various parts of the human body, how they function, and how to take care of them.
ISBN 0-7894-6707-0
1. Body, Human--Juvenile literature. 2. Human anatomy--Juvenile literature. [1. Body, Human. 2. Human anatomy. 3. Human physiology.] I. Title.
QM27 .D39 2000
611--dc21

00-029469

Reproduced by Colourscan, Singapore
Printed and bound in China by L. Rex Printing Co. Ltd

See our complete catalog at
www.dk.com

Contents

Mr S. Skinless
1 Bony Place
Skeletown
Nerveshire

Introduction

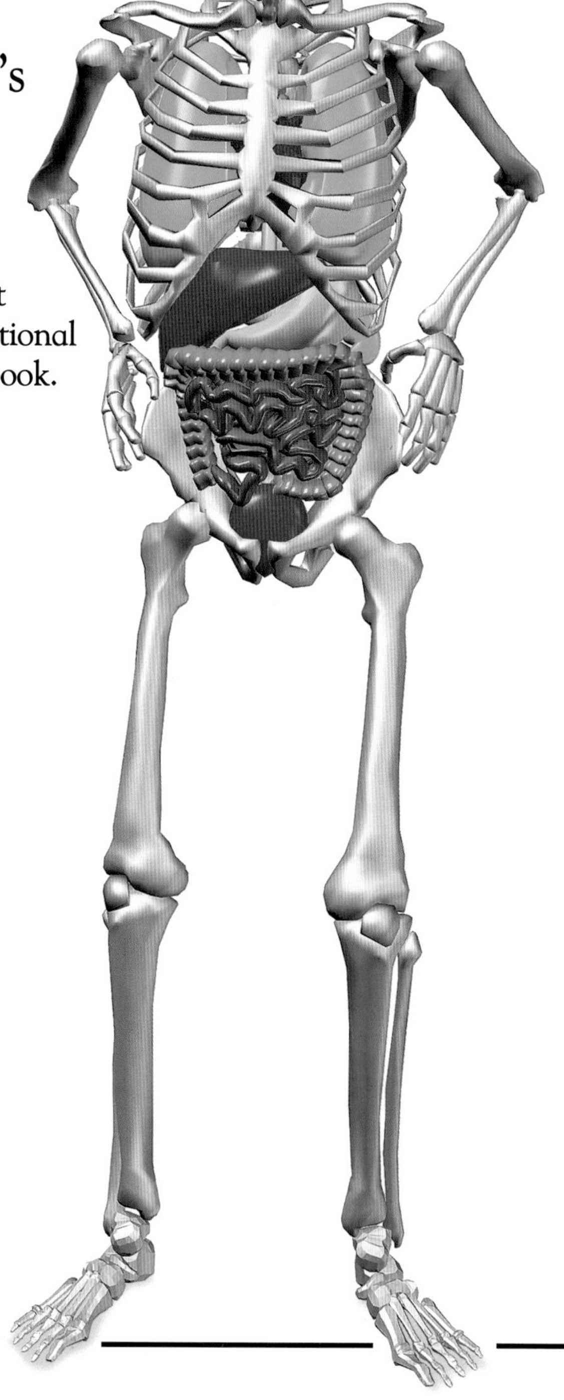

They call me Seemore, because you can SEE MORE of what's inside me! Ha!

Meet Seemore Skinless, the no-skin know-it-all who gives the term "bonehead" a good name! He thinks he knows everything about the human body – an incredibly complex packet of organs that works together to keep you living, growing, and feeling good. But there's a lot more to the body than that.

Seemore's here to help

Throughout the book you'll find "Seemore Says," "Try it Yourself," and "Ask Seemore" boxes. They provide additional information for many of the human body topics in the book.

Ask Seemore

Ask Seemore and he'll do his best to answer the questions that you've always wanted to ask.

Seemore Says

Seemore tells it like it is. Find out more with these information boxes.

Try it Yourself

Try it yourself to put the theories into practice.

This symbol tells you where to look for further information on the *Human Body Explorer* CD-ROM.

Keep an eye out for those curly questions!

Everything's connected in this book. Following the curly questions will take you forward and backward to understand how no part of the body acts alone.

Four books in one

Human Body Explorer is divided into four fact-packed sections – Body Parts, Body Mechanics, Growing-up Guide, and Body Maintenance. Each one looks at the human body in a completely different way.

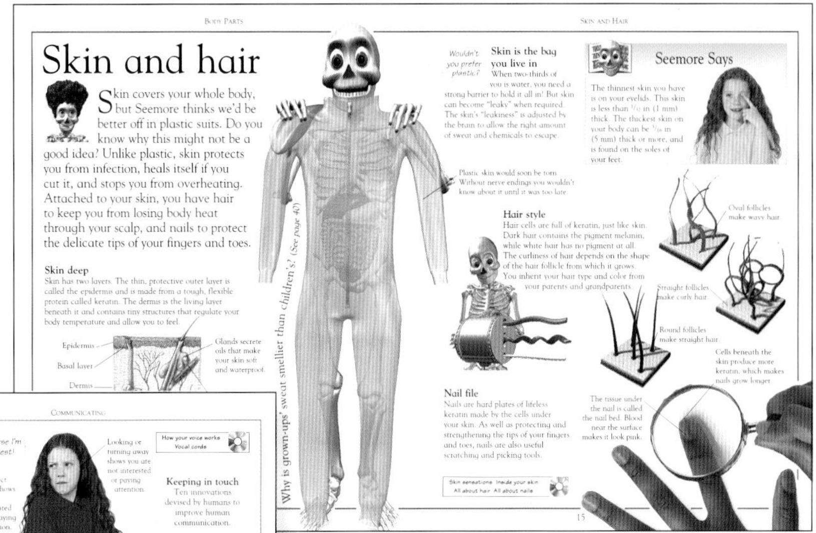

Body Parts

See what's underneath your skin and find out about the body's systems.

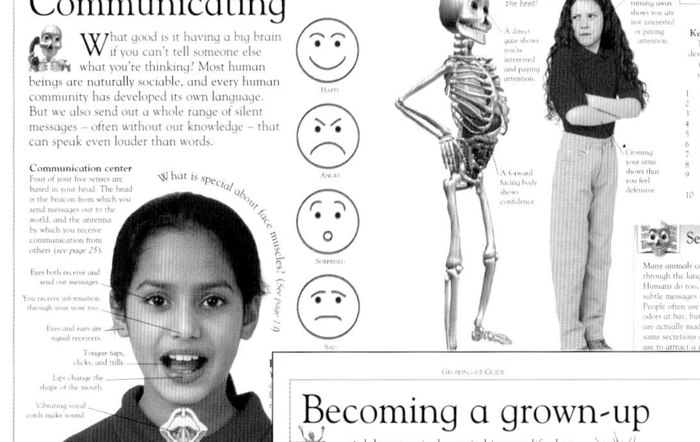

Body Mechanics

Find out how the different systems all work together to make your body operate like a well-designed machine.

Growing-up Guide

Go back in time to discover what it was like to be no bigger than a pinprick. Then look to the future and see what changes lie ahead.

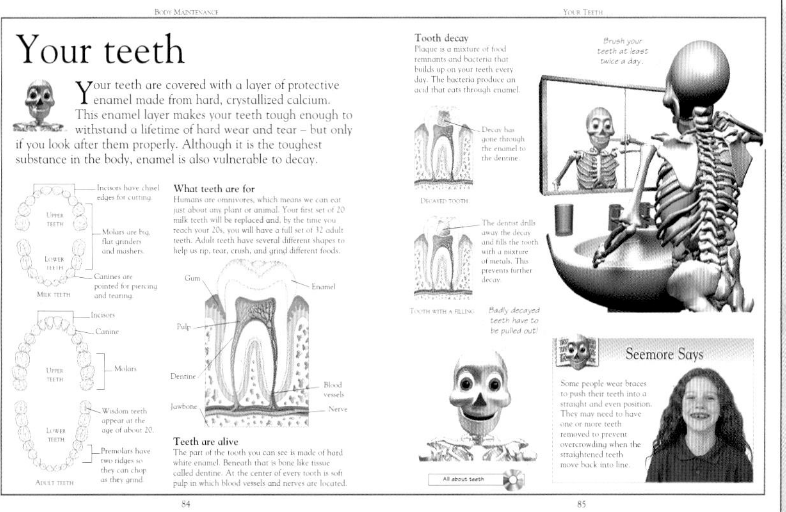

Body Maintenance

You only get one body and what you do with it is up to you. This section has the information you need to choose wisely.

Body parts

Seemore thinks he can make a new friend by building a human body out of raw materials. He has all the ingredients. How hard can it be? All he has to do is make the molecules, then use these to make cells, from which he can create body tissue, which in turn can be used to make the body's organs. No problem!

Actually, it won't be long before Seemore finds out that there's much more to making a body than just mixing all the ingredients together!

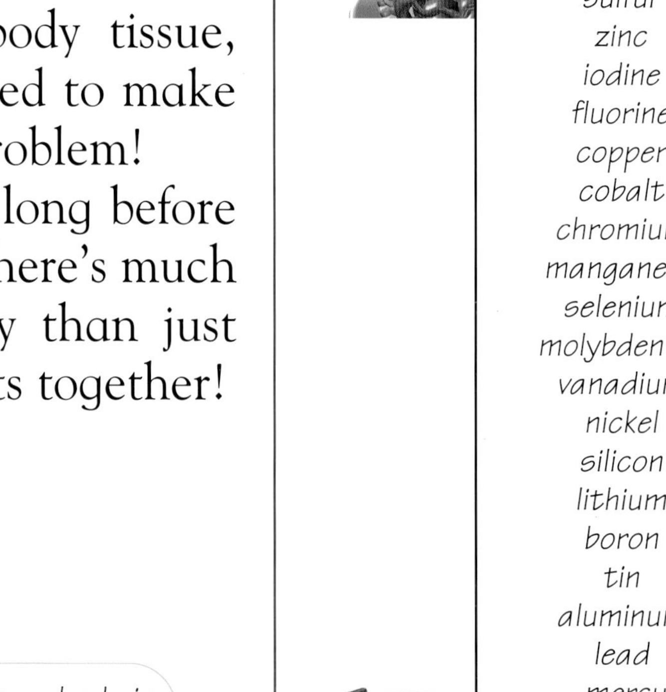

I've got it all here!

Basic ingredients for a human body

carbon
oxygen
hydrogen
nitrogen
calcium
iron
phosphorous
chlorine
sulfur
zinc
iodine
fluorine
copper
cobalt
chromium
manganese
selenium
molybdenum
vanadium
nickel
silicon
lithium
boron
tin
aluminum
lead
mercury
cadmium

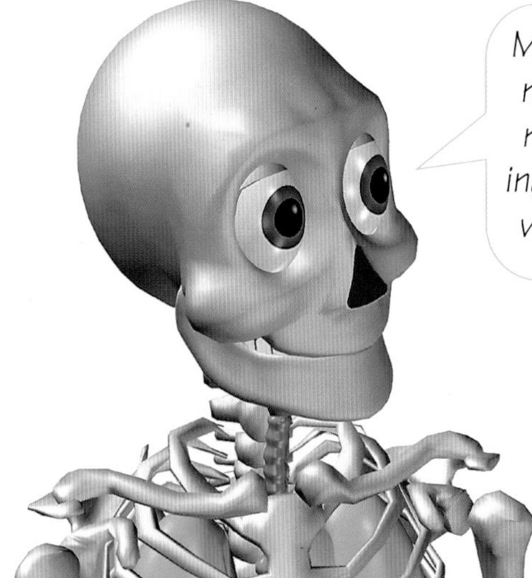

Making a body is no problem. You need the finest ingredients and a very big blender.

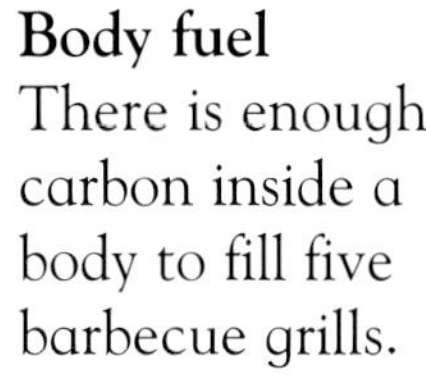

Body fuel
There is enough carbon inside a body to fill five barbecue grills.

Water works
Water is vital for life. A human body contains enough to fill six buckets.

Body fat
The fat in seven big bars of bath soap is roughly the amount of fat in a human body.

Sweet as sugar
There is the equivalent of a small bowlful of sugar inside every human body.

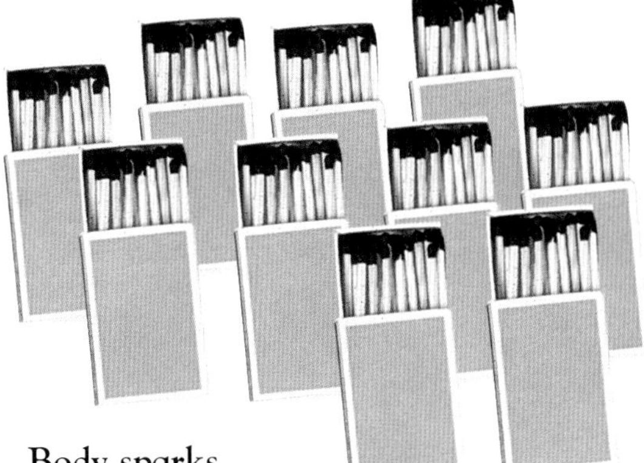

Made of metal
Iron is an essential mineral and the human body contains enough to make one 3 in-long (7 cm-long) nail.

Body sparks
The body contains enough of the mineral phosphorous to make 2,200 matchheads.

Build-a-Buddy
Complete kit
Order now!
Easy to make!
I'm much too busy to pick it up! Do you deliver?

Body by mail

Seemore's given up. He's finally realized that there are easier ways of making friends. He's going to try and make one from a kit that he saw advertised in the newspaper. At least a kit will come with a set of easy-to-follow instructions!

Build a body

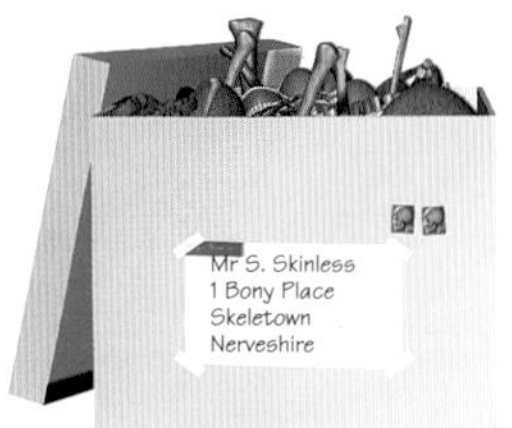

Seemore's body kit has arrived in pieces and Seemore doesn't know where to start. He knows that there are hundreds of parts inside the body – bony ones, squishy ones, even liquid ones. But each part is useless if it's taken out of its system. A system is a group of parts that works together to get a related set of jobs done. There are lots of different systems, and they are all packed together tightly to fit inside the body.

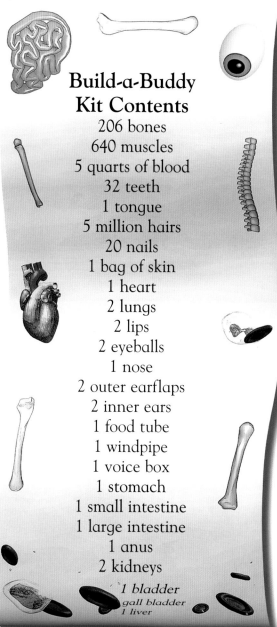

Build-a-Buddy Kit Contents

206 bones
640 muscles
5 quarts of blood
32 teeth
1 tongue
5 million hairs
20 nails
1 bag of skin
1 heart
2 lungs
2 lips
2 eyeballs
1 nose
2 outer earflaps
2 inner ears
1 food tube
1 windpipe
1 voice box
1 stomach
1 small intestine
1 large intestine
1 anus
2 kidneys
1 bladder
gall bladder
1 liver

Seemore Says

Humans are mammals. That means we belong to a group of hair-covered animals that give birth to live young (not eggs). Each species of mammal has a body suited to its lifestyle and environment. We all look very different, but every mammal has the same systems at work inside.

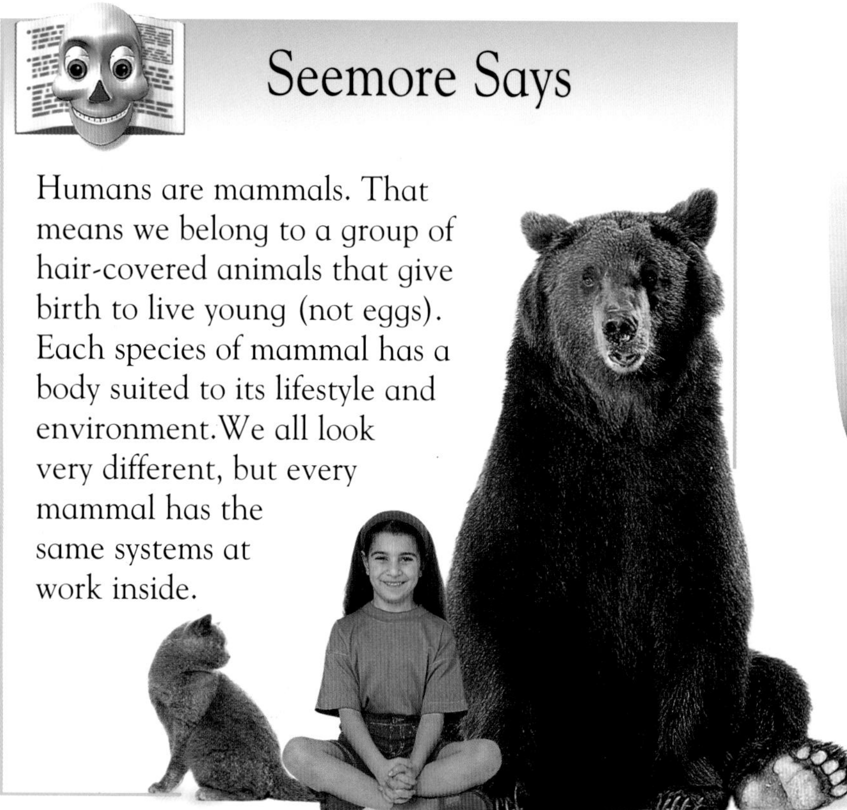

Putting it together

Even a team of top surgeons would find building Seemore's friend difficult. Seemore hasn't got a chance! He needs to find out more about the different parts of the human body. So, buckle your seatbelts as you join him on a voyage of discovery.

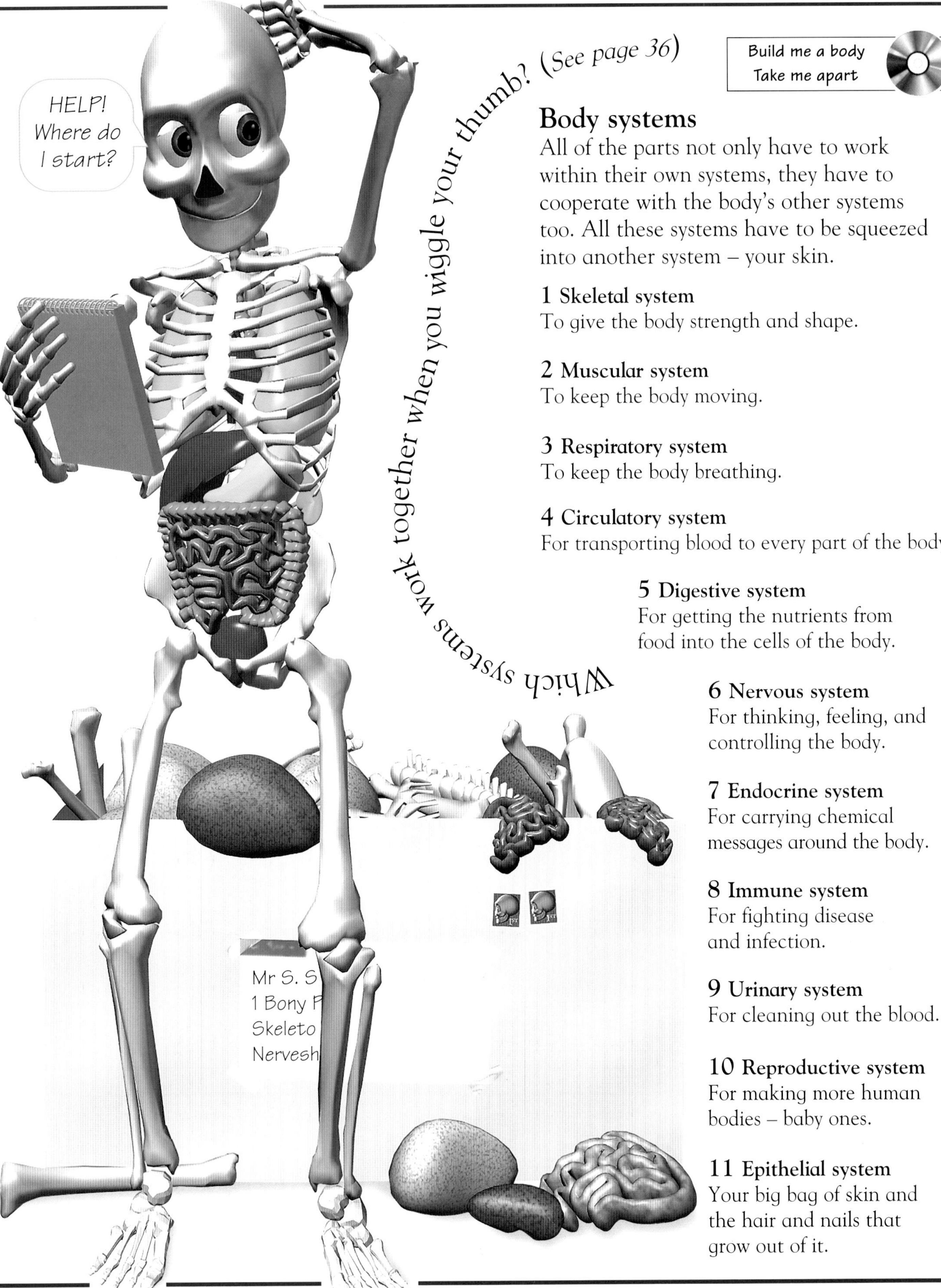

HELP!
Where do
I start?
Mr S. S
1 Bony P
Skeleto
Nervesh
Which systems work together when you wiggle your thumb? (See page 36)
Build me a body
Take me apart

Body systems

All of the parts not only have to work within their own systems, they have to cooperate with the body's other systems too. All these systems have to be squeezed into another system – your skin.

1 Skeletal system
To give the body strength and shape.

2 Muscular system
To keep the body moving.

3 Respiratory system
To keep the body breathing.

4 Circulatory system
For transporting blood to every part of the body.

5 Digestive system
For getting the nutrients from food into the cells of the body.

6 Nervous system
For thinking, feeling, and controlling the body.

7 Endocrine system
For carrying chemical messages around the body.

8 Immune system
For fighting disease and infection.

9 Urinary system
For cleaning out the blood.

10 Reproductive system
For making more human bodies – baby ones.

11 Epithelial system
Your big bag of skin and the hair and nails that grow out of it.

Bony parts

You often see skeletons shown as scary cartoon monsters, or as symbols of doom on pirate flags. But you shouldn't be scared of something that does so many important jobs. The 206 bones of the skeleton hold you up, protect your vital organs, and enable you to move your body using a variety of joints.

There are 22 bones in the skull.

Pivot joint

Shoulder blade

Jawbone

Collar bone

Sternum

Cartilage

12 pairs of ribs

There are 27 bones in each hand.

Humerus

Radius

Ulna

The spine is a stack of separate, rotating vertebrae.

Ball and socket joint

Saddle joint

Hand

The pelvis is wider in women than in men.

Compact bone

Calcium

Milk contains the mineral calcium, which keeps bones straight and strong.

Full of holes

Bones are smooth and hard on the outside, but spongy on the inside. This makes them very strong but not too heavy.

Body joints

In order to move your body, you need joints. Joints are formed where two bones meet. The movement they allow depends on the shape of the bones that form the joint. Some of the main types of joints are explained below. Can you see them on the skeleton?

Hinge joints allow movement forward and backward but not from side to side. Your knee is a good example of a hinge joint.

Ball and socket joints, such as your shoulder, enable bones to swivel. The round end of one bone fits inside the cup-shaped socket of the other.

Saddle joints connect your thumbs to your hands. They allow you to move your thumbs in lots of different directions.

Pivot joints are found between the vertebrae in your neck. They enable the bones to rotate.

Ligaments

Ligaments are the strong, flexible straps that hold your bones together.

Bone

Ligament

The hip is a ball and socket joint.

The thigh bone, or femur, is the longest bone in the body.

Kneecap

How do bones mend themselves? (See page 45)

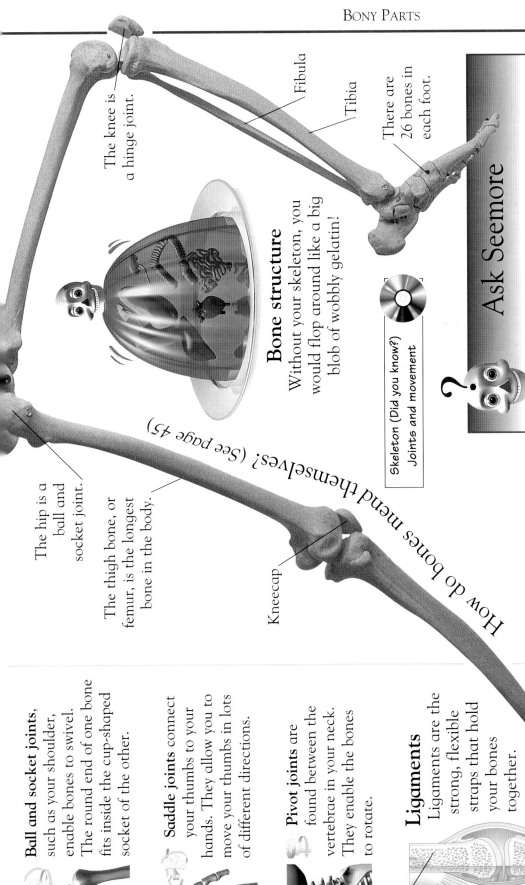

The knee is a hinge joint.

Fibula

Tibia

There are 26 bones in each foot.

Bone structure

Without your skeleton, you would flop around like a big blob of wobbly gelatin!

Skeleton (Did you know?)
Joints and movement

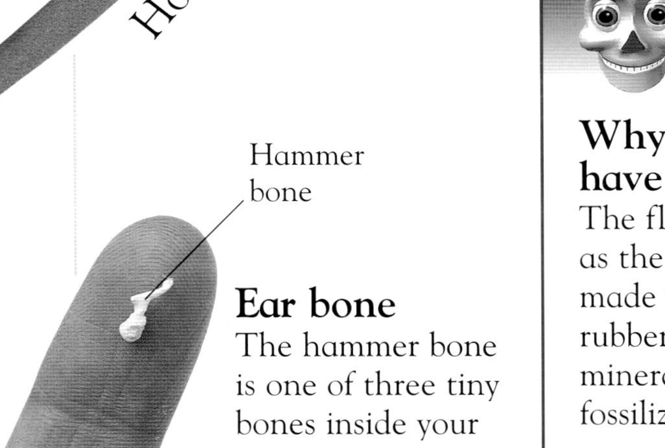

Hammer bone

Ear bone

The hammer bone is one of three tiny bones inside your ear (*see page 25*).

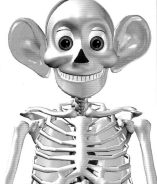

Ask Seemore

Why don't skeletons have ears?

The flappy outer ear, as well as the end of your nose, is made from cartilage. It's a rubbery tissue without many minerals, so it doesn't fossilize the way bone does.

Muscly parts

Every time you blink your eyes or wiggle your toes, you move your muscles. Every time your heart beats, you're moving more muscles. The skeletal muscles are the "meat on your bones." You have 640 of them, and they account for around 40% of your body's weight.

The trapezius muscles move your shoulder blades.

Gluteus maximus

The hamstring muscles bend your knee.

The muscle at the front of your thigh straightens your knee

The gastrocnemius, or calf muscle, moves your lower leg.

Why do muscles feel firm when they're at rest? (See page 37)

The deltoid muscle in your shoulder helps you raise your arm.

The masseter muscle exerts a crushing force when closing the jaw.

Pectoral muscles move your shoulder and upper arm.

Abdominal muscles strengthen your upper body and protect your internal organs.

Biggest muscle

Your biggest muscle is the gluteus maximus in your bottom. It straightens your leg, helps you climb the stairs, and makes an excellent cushion!

Muscly organs

The organs inside your body are muscular, too. They are controlled automatically by your brain, even while you're asleep. The muscles of your heart never stop working your whole life long.

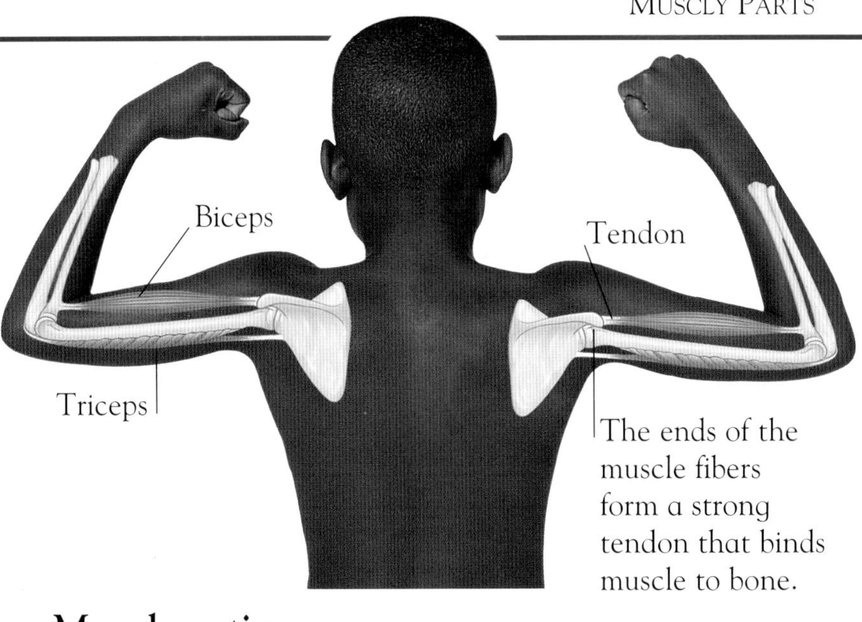

The ends of the muscle fibers form a strong tendon that binds muscle to bone.

Face muscles

Face muscles are special because they tug your skin rather than your bones. When you smile or make a funny face, you actually use about 30 different muscles. Your most active muscles are those that move your eyeballs in their sockets.

Muscle action

As the biceps muscle contracts (gets shorter and fatter) to bend your arm, the triceps muscle relaxes (gets longer and thinner). In order to straighten your arm again, the biceps muscle relaxes while the triceps muscle contracts.

Muscle fibers

Under the microscope, the striped pattern of muscle fibers is clearly visible. Nerve impulses run between the fibers to make your muscles contract when your brain tells them to (*see page 37*).

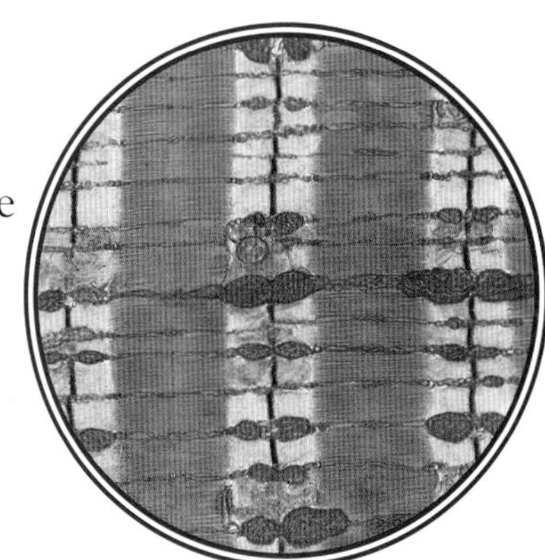

It's not fair! I don't even have muscles!

Try it Yourself

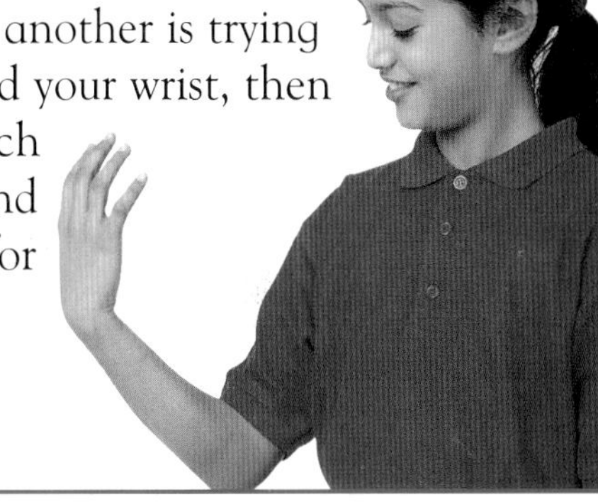

One muscle can interfere with what another is trying to do. Bend your wrist, then try to clench your fist and you'll see for yourself.

Tug of war

The most powerful muscles are the ones that run along your spine. These hold your body up all day, and are essential for jobs like lifting and rope pulling. The smallest skeletal muscle you have is in your inner ear. It moves the smallest bone in your body to help adjust your hearing to changes in volume.

Joints and movement
Muscle (fact file) All about muscle
How muscles and bones work

Skin and hair

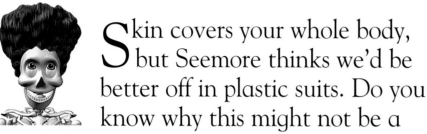

Skin covers your whole body, but Seemore thinks we'd be better off in plastic suits. Do you know why this might not be a good idea? Unlike plastic, skin protects you from infection, heals itself if you cut it, and stops you from overheating. Attached to your skin, you have hair to keep you from losing body heat through your scalp, and nails to protect the delicate tips of your fingers and toes.

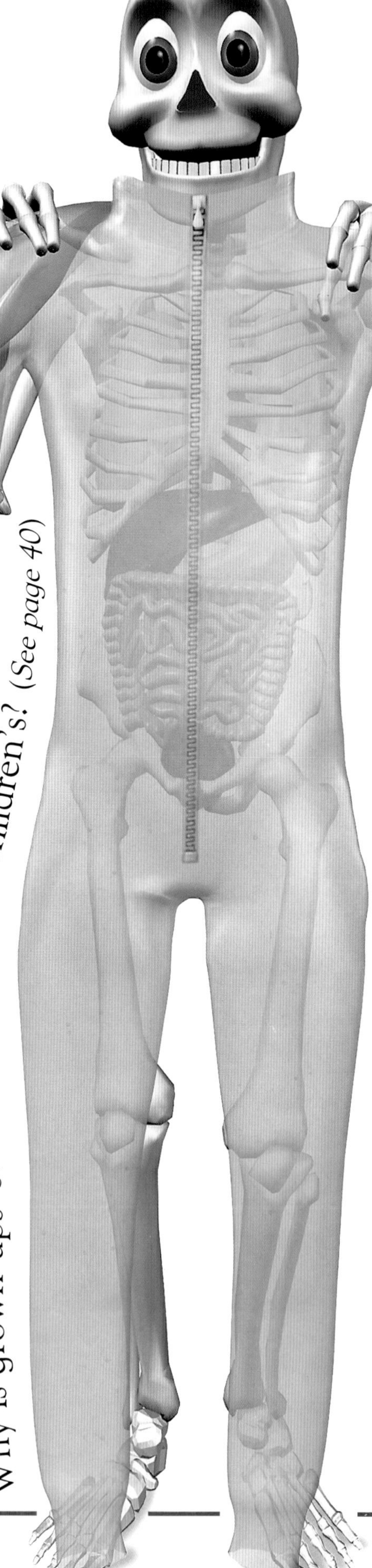

Why is grown-ups' sweat smellier than children's? (See page 40)

Skin deep

Skin has two layers. The thin, protective outer layer is called the epidermis and is made from a tough, flexible protein called keratin. The dermis is the living layer beneath it and contains tiny structures that regulate your body temperature and allow you to feel.

Epidermis

Basal layer

Dermis

Sweat glands send water to the skin's surface to cool it down (*see page 40*).

Nerve endings allow you to feel heat, pain, and pressure.

Glands secrete oils that make your skin soft and waterproof.

When it's cold, tiny muscles pull the hairs straight up and form goose pimples.

A layer of fat provides insulation and cushions the bones beneath.

Wouldn't you prefer plastic?

Skin is the bag you live in

When two-thirds of you is water, you need a strong barrier to hold it all in! But skin can become "leaky" when required. The skin's "leakiness" is adjusted by the brain to allow the right amount of sweat and chemicals to escape.

Seemore Says

The thinnest skin you have is on your eyelids. This skin is less than 1/32 in (1 mm) thick. The thickest skin on your body can be 3/16 in (5 mm) thick or more, and is found on the soles of your feet.

Plastic skin would soon be torn. Without nerve endings you wouldn't know about it until it was too late.

Hair style

Hair cells are full of keratin, just like skin. Dark hair contains the pigment melanin, while white hair has no pigment at all. The curliness of hair depends on the shape of the hair follicle from which it grows. You inherit your hair type and color from your parents and grandparents.

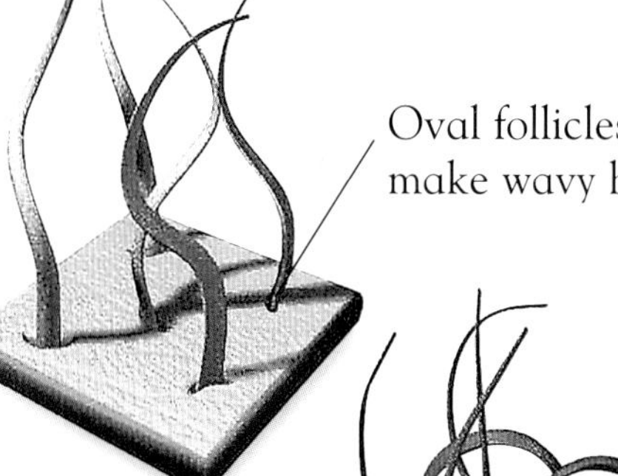

Oval follicles make wavy hair.

Straight follicles make curly hair.

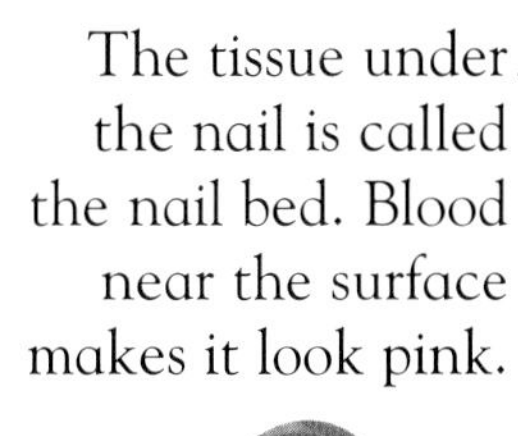

Round follicles make straight hair.

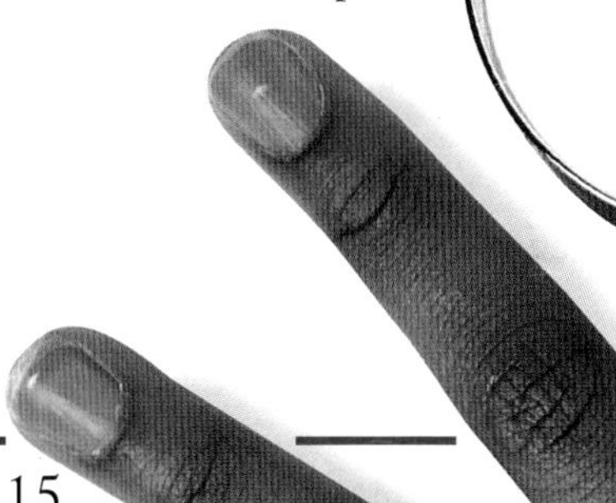

Cells beneath the skin produce more keratin, which makes nails grow longer.

The tissue under the nail is called the nail bed. Blood near the surface makes it look pink.

Nail file

Nails are hard plates of lifeless keratin made by the cells under your skin. As well as protecting and strengthening the tips of your fingers and toes, nails are also useful scratching and picking tools.

Skin sensations Inside your skin
All about hair All about nails

Breathing parts

Good gas in. Bad gas out. It's a 24-hour job keeping your body supplied with oxygen and getting rid of carbon dioxide waste. Your lungs form a gas exchange area, moving fresh air in and stale air out of your bloodstream. Pumping the air in and out is done by a huge muscle, the diaphragm, which spans all the way across your middle.

Trachea

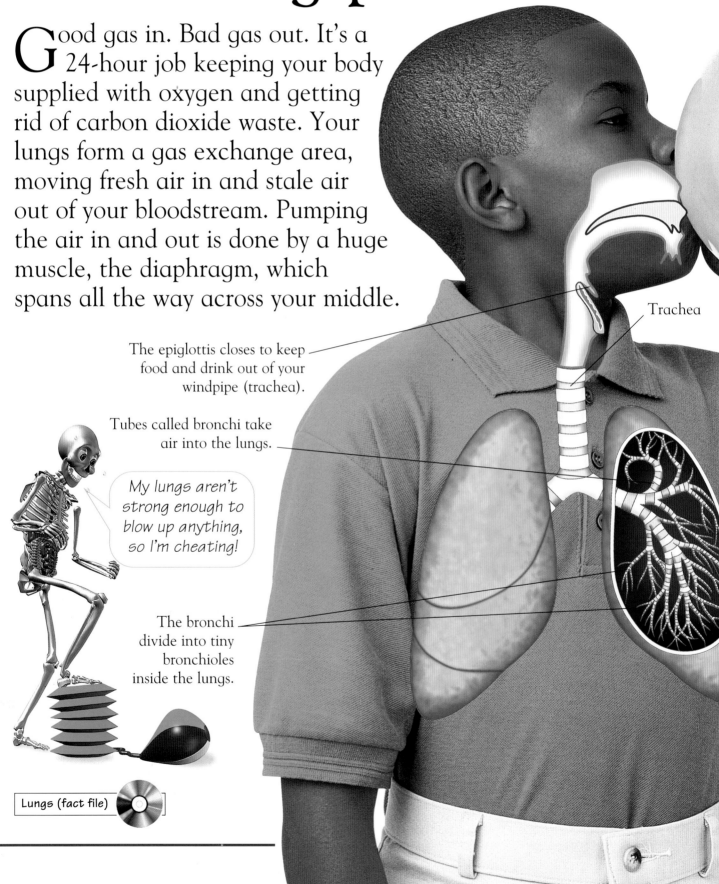

The epiglottis closes to keep food and drink out of your windpipe (trachea).

Tubes called bronchi take air into the lungs.

My lungs aren't strong enough to blow up anything, so I'm cheating!

The bronchi divide into tiny bronchioles inside the lungs.

Lungs (fact file)

Why do we need oxygen? (See pages 38–39)

Pass the gas

Your lungs are more than just a pair of windbags! They're made of thousands of tiny sacs called alveoli, whose thin walls allow oxygen and carbon dioxide to pass in and out of the surrounding blood vessels.

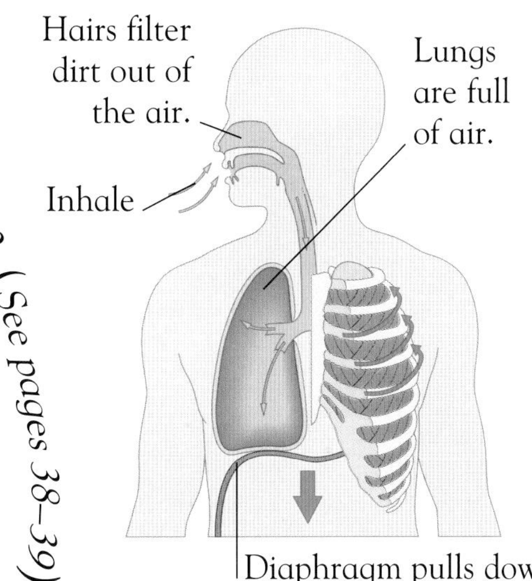

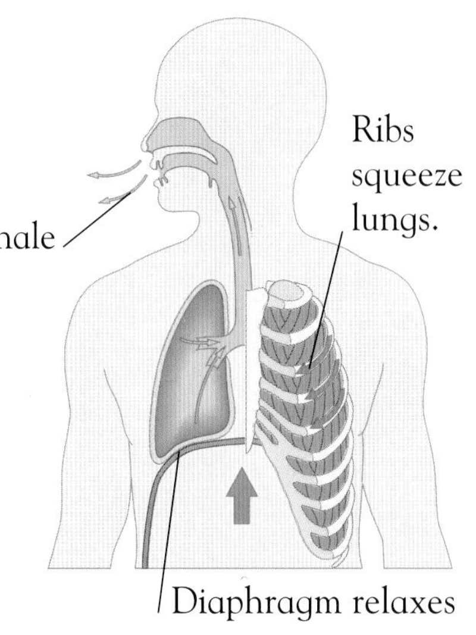

Breathing in

Air is carried to the lungs by a network of smaller and smaller tubes. The diaphragm lowers to allow the lungs to fill with air.

Breathing out

The diaphragm relaxes and the ribs push down on the lungs, pushing stale air out. The lungs get smaller.

What a gas!

The air we breathe is a mixture of gas molecules and tiny particles. They're present in roughly the proportions shown by this beach ball chart.

Water provides humidity.

Airborne particles such as smoke, dust, pollen, and even germs!

Carbon dioxide is essential for plants.

Oxygen is essential for animal life.

Nitrogen dilutes the oxygen.

Alveoli

The alveoli at the ends of the bronchioles are wrapped in tiny blood vessels. If spread out, the surface area of these sacs would be about 753 sq. ft. (70 m^2).

Seemore Says

In your lifetime, you're likely to breathe out enough air to inflate 138 hot-air balloons.

Bloody parts

Build me a body Heart
Search heart/blood What am I made of?

Inside your body there is a network of transport canals that moves food, messages, and building supplies to the places they're needed most. This is the circulatory system through which your blood flows. The blood is the only organ in the body that's a fluid. Grown-ups have about five quarts (five liters) of the stuff, and it's kept moving by a powerful and tireless pump – the heart.

If your blood vessels were joined together, they would circle the Earth TWICE!

Blood from the veins is bluish in color.

Blood capillaries

Capillaries are the tiny vessels that connect arteries and veins. Their thin walls allow oxygen, nutrients, and waste to pass in and out of the bloodstream.

Red arteries and blue veins

You have three kinds of blood vessels in your body: arteries that carry red, oxygen-rich blood away from the heart; veins that bring bluish, oxygen-poor blood back to the heart; and capillaries.

Heart chambers

Your heart has four chambers – two on the left and two on the right. The right atrium collects deoxygenated blood from the body, and the right ventricle pumps the stale blood to the lungs to be oxygenated. The left atrium collects the oxygen-rich blood from the lungs, and the left ventricle pumps the fresh blood at high pressure out to the rest of the body.

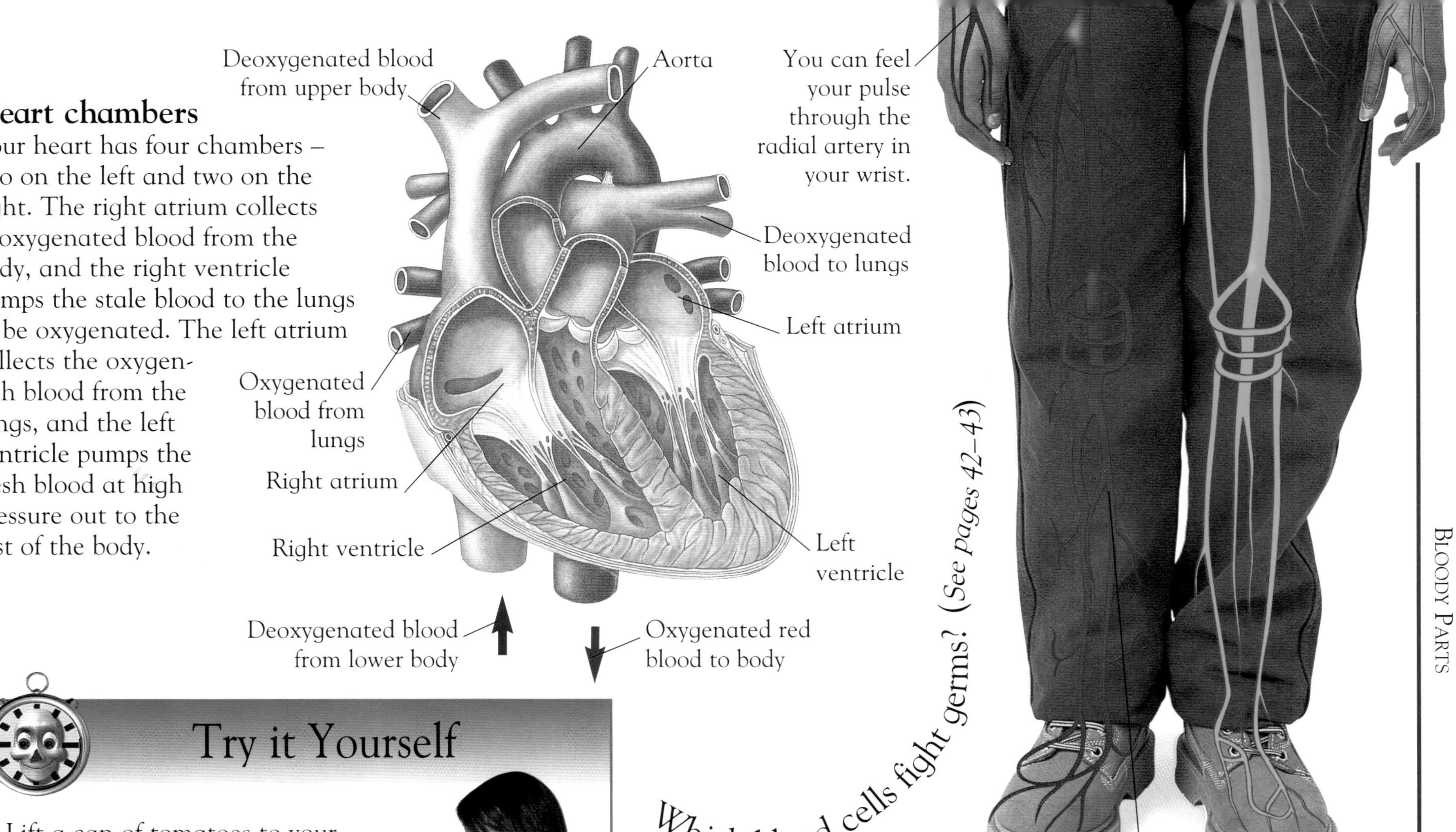

Which blood cells fight germs? (See pages 42–43)

Try it Yourself

Lift a can of tomatoes to your shoulder. That's about how much work your heart does with every beat. Now try lifting that can 70 times a minute. Make that 140 times in two minutes. Now imagine lifting that can every minute of your life. That's how hard your heart has to work!

Blue to red

Red blood cells contain a protein called hemoglobin which turns red when an oxygen molecule binds to it. The iron you get from vegetables is used to make new hemoglobin.

Gutsy parts

Whenever you eat something, the food is processed by the organs of the digestive system. It's only about a 26-foot (8-meter) journey through your body from the cereal bowl to the toilet bowl, so your body needs to get as many nutrients out of each mouthful as it possibly can.

Is it true that you are what you eat? (See pages 30–31)

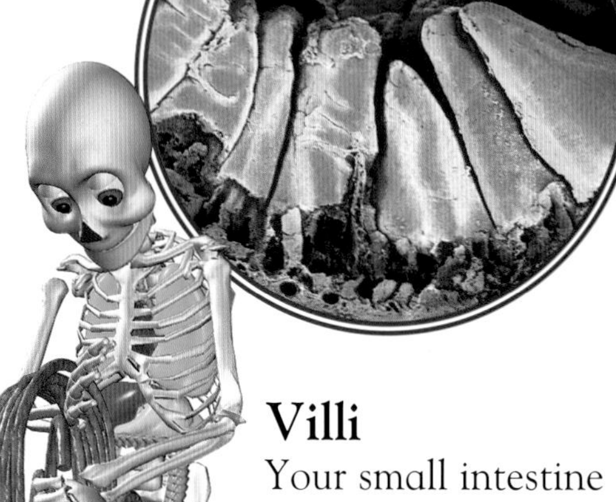

Villi

Your small intestine (see opposite) is about 16 feet (five meters) long and lined on the inside with tiny furlike cells called villi. The villi absorb nutrients from your food. Inside the villi are tiny capillaries through which food passes into the bloodstream and circulates around your body.

How many elephants can you eat?

In your lifetime you'll eat around 66,000 lb (30,000 kg) of food – the weight of six elephants. Fortunately for your digestive system, you'll eat it all in slightly smaller portions!

Seemore Says

The surface area of the villi inside your small intestine is large enough to cover a tennis court. The large surface area allows rapid absorption of water and nutrients.

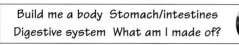

Build me a body Stomach/intestines
Digestive system What am I made of?

The process of digestion

The digestive system is made up of the long tube that runs from your mouth to your anus, together with the digestive organs. These organs include the salivary glands, the liver, and the pancreas.

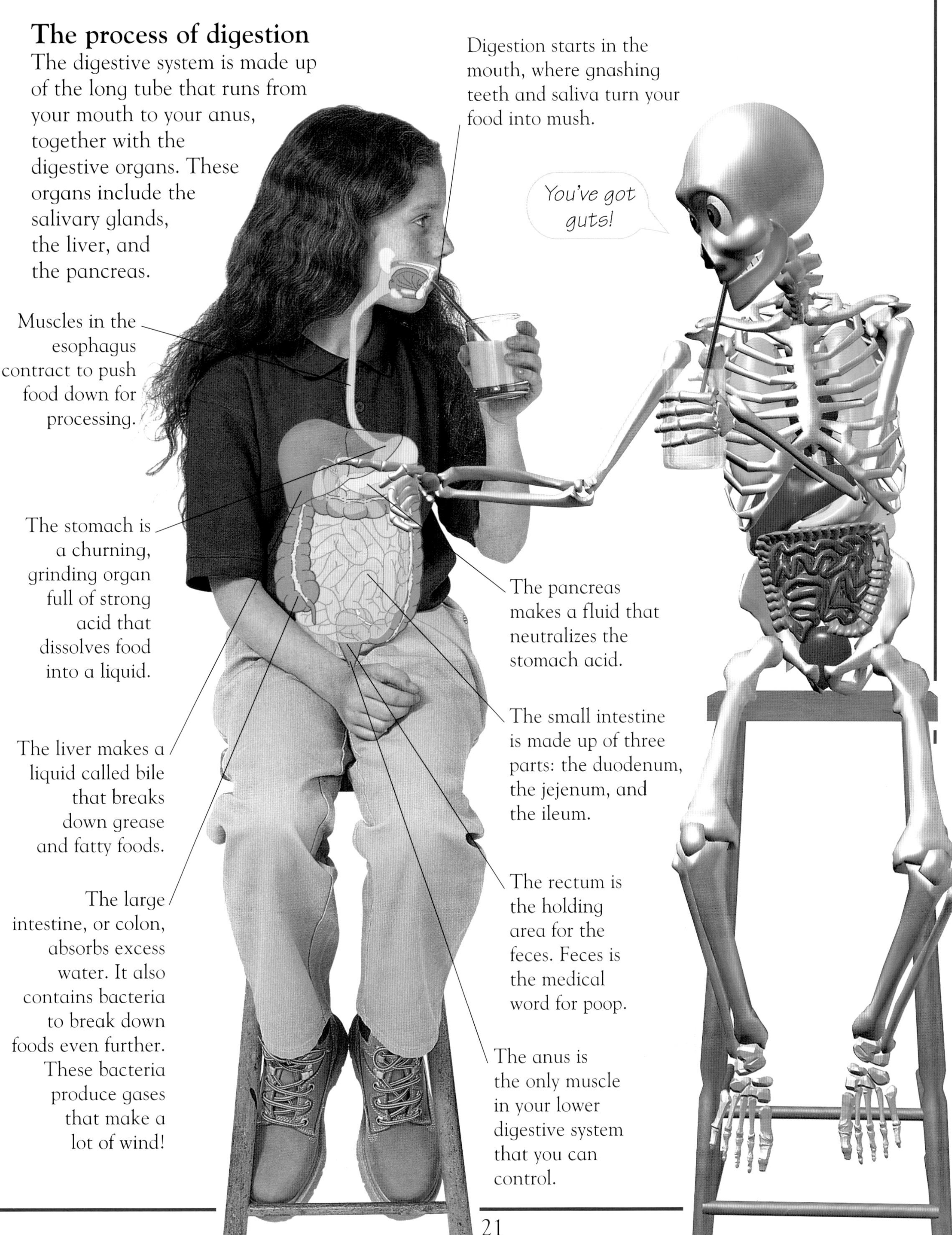

Digestion starts in the mouth, where gnashing teeth and saliva turn your food into mush.

Muscles in the esophagus contract to push food down for processing.

The stomach is a churning, grinding organ full of strong acid that dissolves food into a liquid.

The liver makes a liquid called bile that breaks down grease and fatty foods.

The large intestine, or colon, absorbs excess water. It also contains bacteria to break down foods even further. These bacteria produce gases that make a lot of wind!

The pancreas makes a fluid that neutralizes the stomach acid.

The small intestine is made up of three parts: the duodenum, the jejenum, and the ileum.

The rectum is the holding area for the feces. Feces is the medical word for poop.

The anus is the only muscle in your lower digestive system that you can control.

Brainy parts

What's 85% water and looks like a giant gray walnut? It's the brain! Brain tissue comes in two colors – gray and white. The gray matter is made from neurons, which do all of your thinking and feeling. The white matter is made from other kinds of cells which support and protect the neurons and their connections.

Which side of the brain does the creative thinking? (See page 47)

Outer brain

A fully grown brain weighs about $4\frac{1}{2}$ lb (1.4 kg) and floats in special nourishing fluid, which helps protect it from damage. Different areas of the brain control different functions. Thinking, moving, and feeling occur in the large outer section of the brain, called the cerebrum. Your memory is controlled from many different parts of the brain.

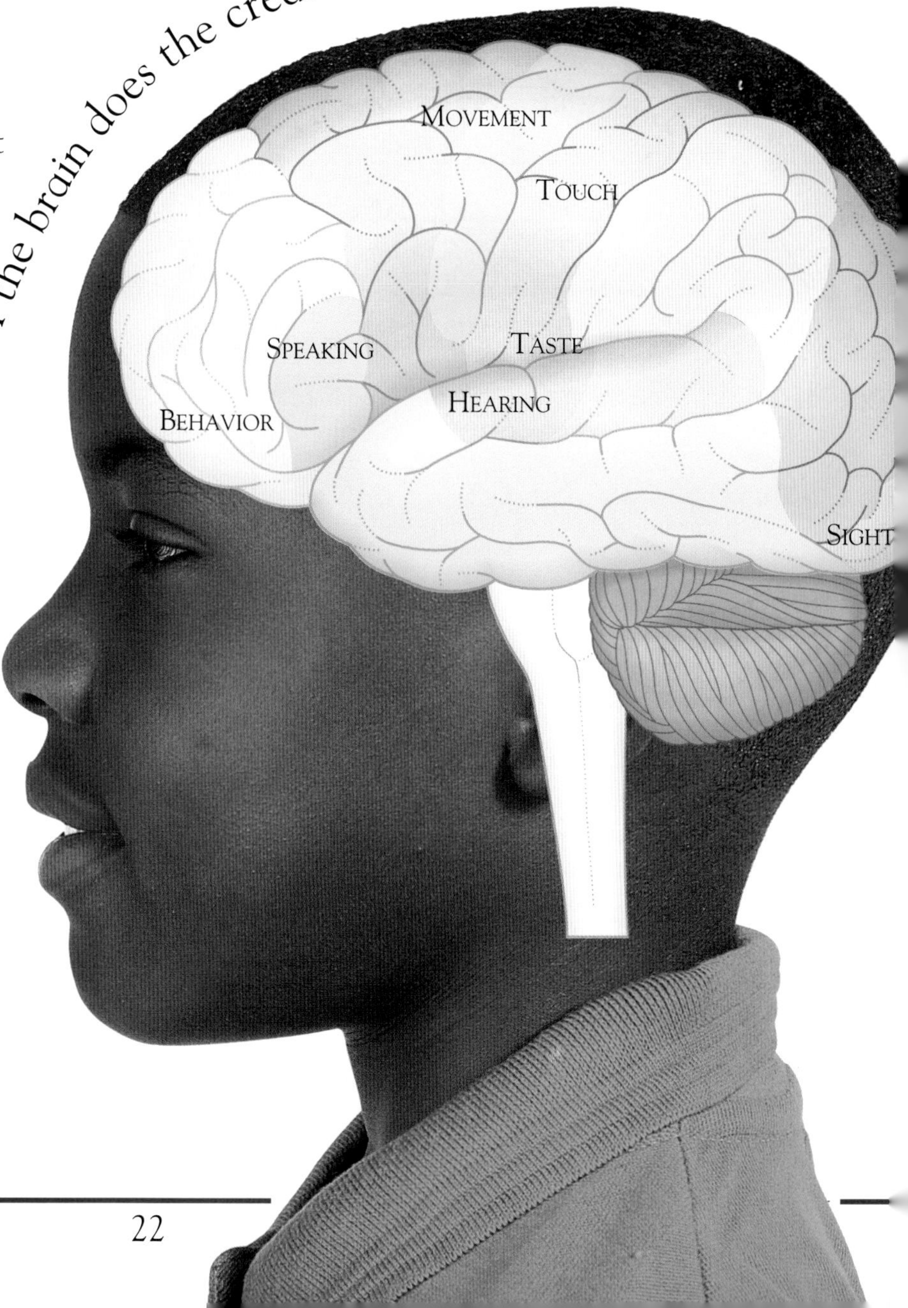

Movement
Touch
Speaking
Taste
Hearing
Behavior
Sight

Ask a friend a math question. Watch which side their eyes move to as they think. Then ask them what color goes with green. People's eyes often move to the left or right as they use each of the hemispheres (sides) of their brains.

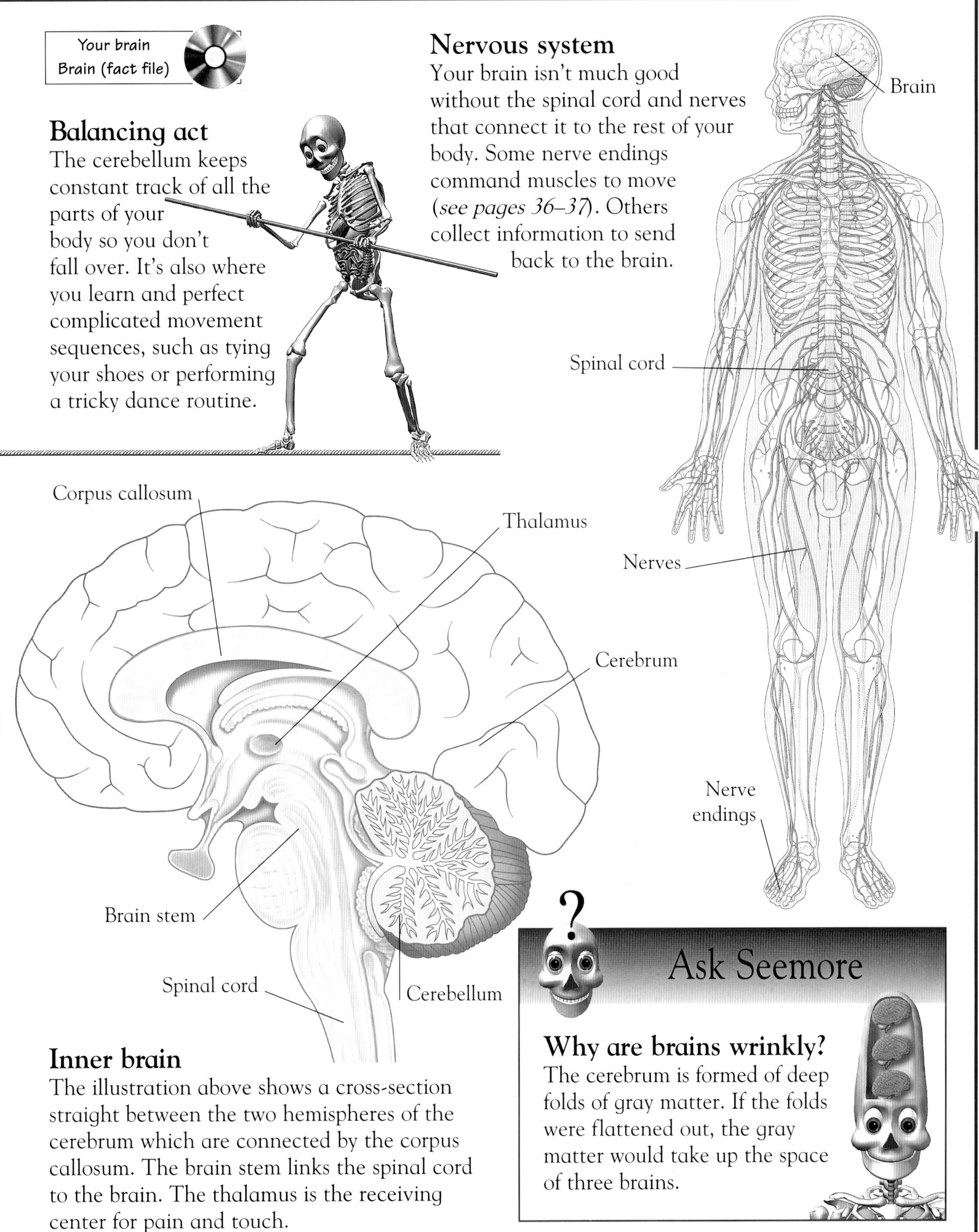

Balancing act

The cerebellum keeps constant track of all the parts of your body so you don't fall over. It's also where you learn and perfect complicated movement sequences, such as tying your shoes or performing a tricky dance routine.

Nervous system

Your brain isn't much good without the spinal cord and nerves that connect it to the rest of your body. Some nerve endings command muscles to move (*see pages 36–37*). Others collect information to send back to the brain.

Inner brain

The illustration above shows a cross-section straight between the two hemispheres of the cerebrum which are connected by the corpus callosum. The brain stem links the spinal cord to the brain. The thalamus is the receiving center for pain and touch.

Ask Seemore

Why are brains wrinkly?

The cerebrum is formed of deep folds of gray matter. If the folds were flattened out, the gray matter would take up the space of three brains.

Sensitive parts

You have five senses to help you discover what's going on around you – sight, sound, taste, smell, and touch. Every animal relies on its senses to find food and avoid danger. Humans use their senses for much more. From enjoying our favorite music to recognizing a friendly face, our senses provide a constant stream of information and stimulation.

Try it Yourself

Ever tried to thread a needle with one eye closed? You need both eyes open to tell you what's near and what's far away from you.

Sight to see

Seventy-five percent of all the information that reaches your brain enters as light. Thanks to their incredible sensitivity, your eyes are more versatile than even the most sophisticated cameras. The nerve endings in the retina translate the focused picture into a pattern of electrical impulses and send them to the brain.

Muscle

The lens is either stretched or squashed by eye muscles to keep the image in focus.

The retina is a screen of light-sensitive nerve endings.

The cornea is a tough, transparent covering.

Optic nerve to brain

The pupil is the opening in the front of your eye.

Muscle

The image is projected upside down.

The iris comes in several colors. It opens wide when the lights are low.

The eye is filled with a clear substance called the vitreous humor.

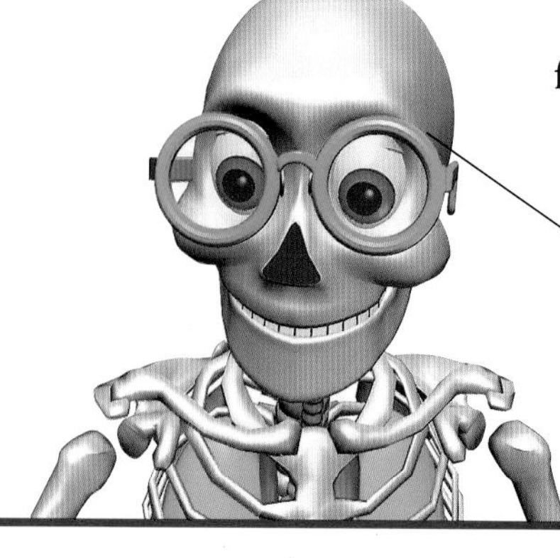

People need to wear glasses when the muscles inside their eyes can't focus the image sharply on the retina.

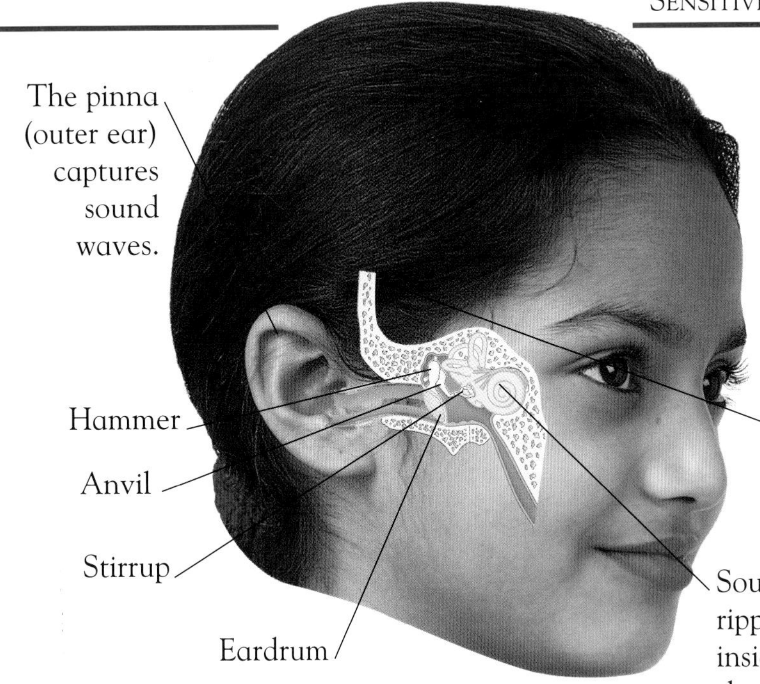

The pinna (outer ear) captures sound waves.
Hammer
Anvil
Stirrup
Eardrum
Electrical signals are sent to the brain.
Sound vibrations ripple the fluid inside your snail-shaped cochlea.

Sound receptors

Sound waves are tiny vibrations in the air. These vibrations are picked up by the eardrum, transferred along a series of three tiny bones, and then passed into the cochlea which is lined with receptor cells that are linked to your brain.

Sensory cells line the inside of your nose.

Smells are carried by airborne particles which enter your nostrils.

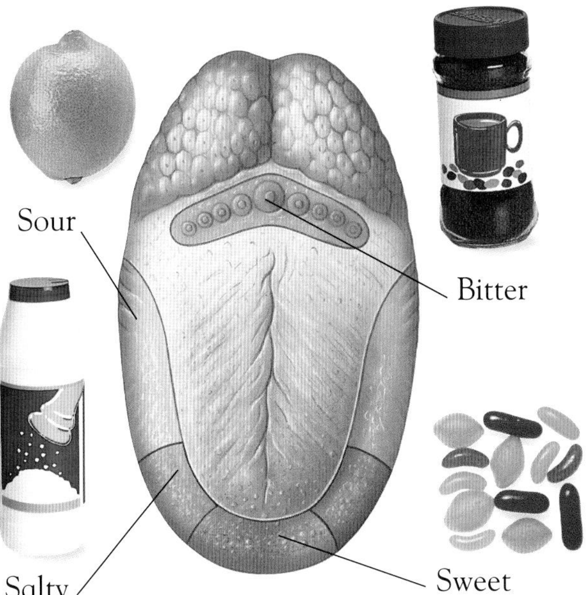

Smell detection

You can detect around 5,000 different scents through the cells that line the inside of your nose. These cells send messages back to your brain to help you identify each smell.

Taste sensation

Tastebuds are tiny receptors on your tongue that allow you to taste what you eat. The tongue is divided into regions as shown above. Each region has only one kind of tastebud and is sensitive to only one taste: sweet, sour, salty, or bitter.

Touch and feel

Your largest sense organ is your skin. The most sensitive parts of your skin have the most nerve endings. These include your tongue, lips, and fingertips.

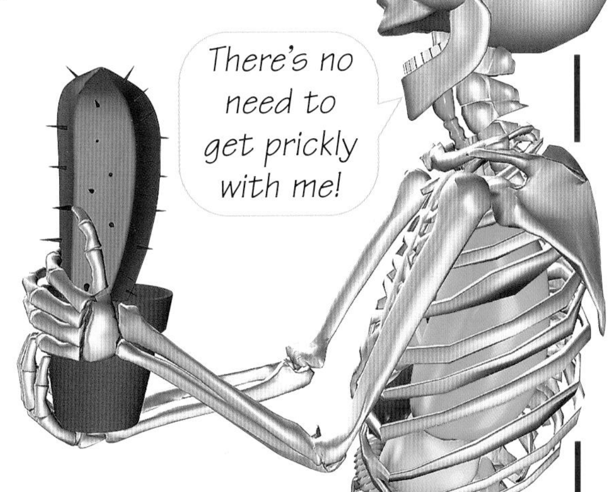

There's no need to get prickly with me!

Eyes and seeing Ears and hearing
Tongue and tasting
Taste the foods Skin and touching

Private parts

Don't blush, Seemore. We all have a urinary system, and most animals, including humans, have either male or female organs. These organs make up the reproductive system, which is used by grown-up humans to make more little humans. Female reproductive organs are on the inside, where they may one day carry and protect a baby. Male reproductive organs are on the outside of the body.

Urinary system

The urinary system is a close neighbor of the reproductive system. In boys' bodies, the two even share the same piping. Your kidneys filter out unwanted water and chemicals from the blood to create urine. Urine is stored in the bladder. When the bladder is full, pressure sensors in the bladder wall tell you it's time to go!

When it's time to go, it's time to go!

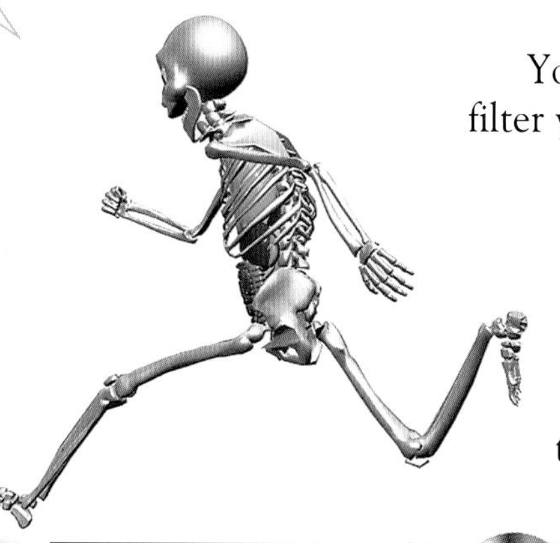

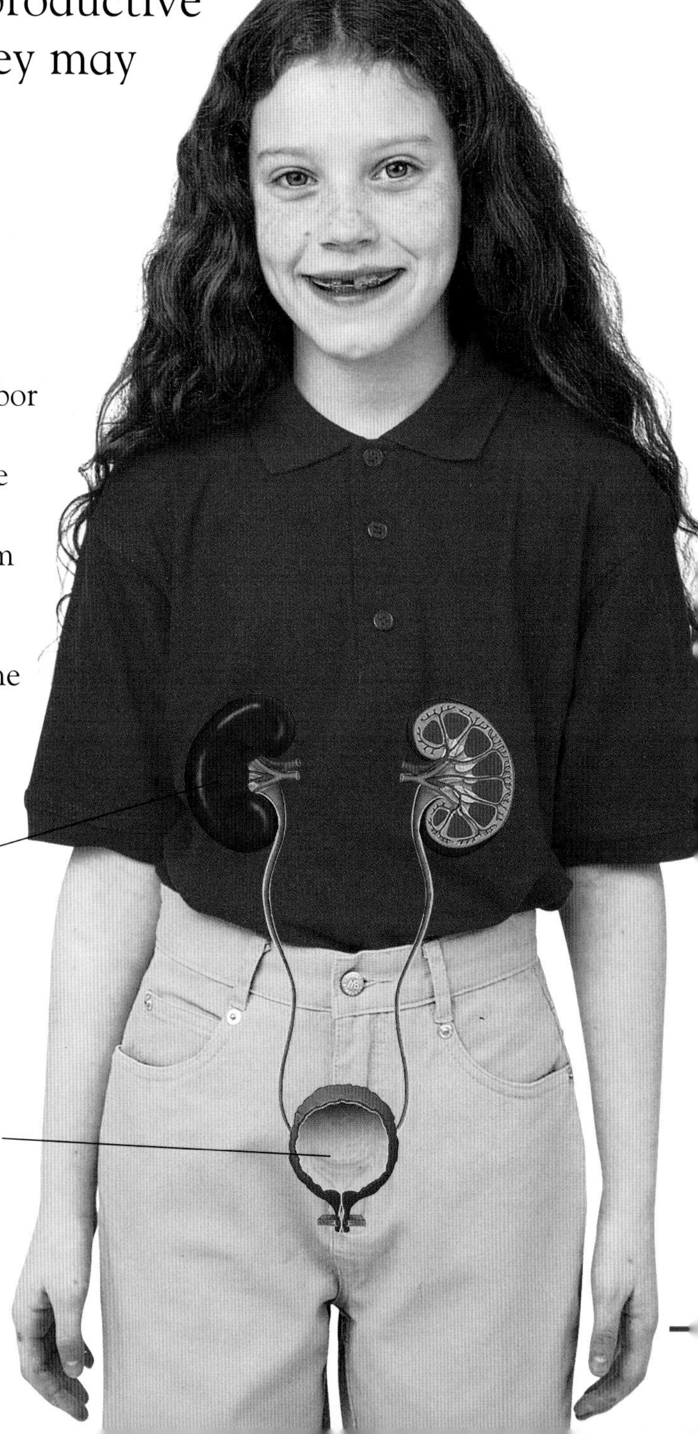

Your kidneys filter your blood.

Urine is stored in a muscular bag called the bladder.

Your urinary system
Where babies come from

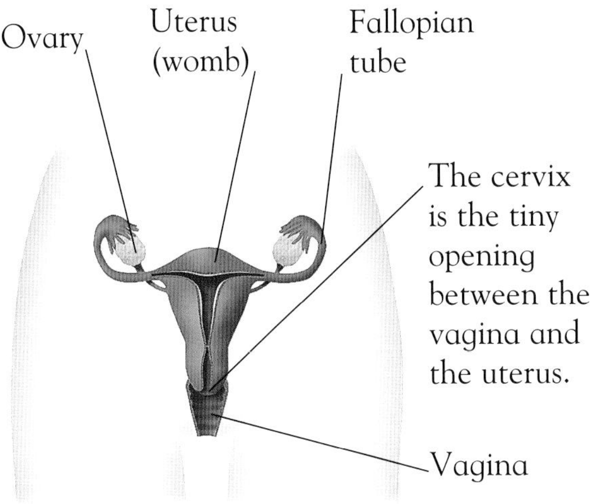

Female organs

All of a woman's eggs are stored in her ovaries. Once she's reached puberty, her ovaries will take turns to release one egg per month into the fallopian tubes, where they will be wafted by microscopic hairlike cells toward the uterus.

A new life

When a man and woman make love, they can make a new life as well. The penis enters the vagina, where it releases sperm-filled semen. If a single sperm enters an egg in the fallopian tube, it is the beginning of an incredible process that results in a new baby.

The cell nucleus is full of genetic information.

The tip of each sperm is packed with energy to power its swim to the egg.

The tail of the sperm is called the flagellum.

What happens when a sperm meets an egg? (See page 54)

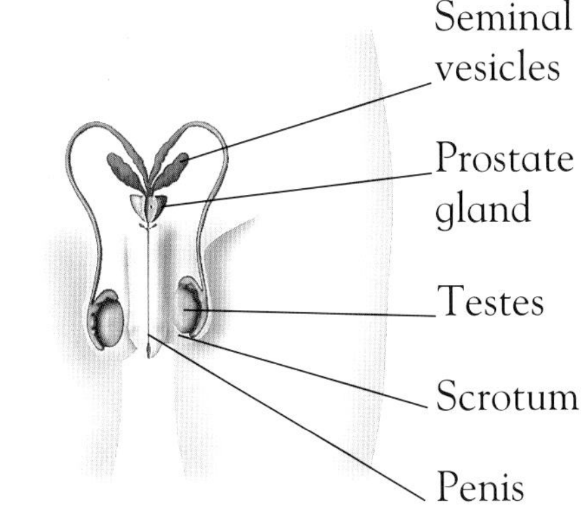

Male organs

Every day, the two testes create about 300 million new sperm. The testes are outside the main part of the body because sperm require cooler temperatures. The prostate gland and seminal vesicles create the sperm-carrying fluid called semen.

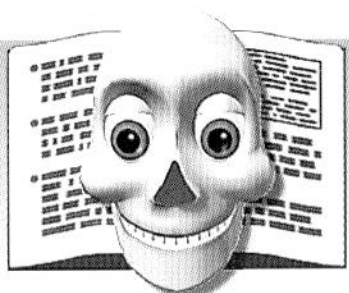

Seemore Says

Ovaries and testes have a lot in common. They're about the same size and shape, they both come in pairs, and they are both responsible for the creation of sex cells (eggs and sperm). Both grow from the same small cluster of cells that come together in the very first week of life. A female baby is born with all the eggs she will ever have already stored in her two ovaries. That's around 200,000 in all.

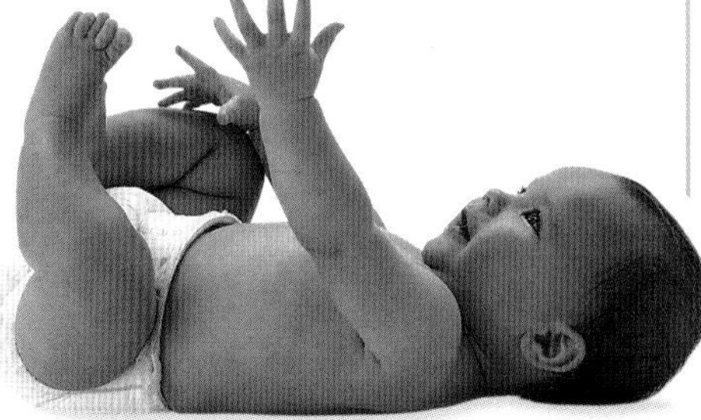

Body mechanics

Brain power
No computer can match your brain for creativity and problem-solving ability.

Look around your home and you'll see tools and machines of all kinds. There are simple ones, like wrenches, that have one function. Others, like cars, can perform several operations at once. But not one of them is as complex and amazing as the machine you live in – your body. From your head to your toes, every single cell of you does its part to keep you alive and kicking.

This section takes you a step further from looking at the basic components of your body. Now, find out how your body systems work together to regulate its temperature, process its fuel, protect itself from germs, and repair itself.

Effective communication
Unlike a radio, you don't communicate by just making sounds. You smile, frown, change your expression, and use body language.

So I won't be needing my tool box?

Amazing adaptability
There hasn't been a vehicle yet that's as "all-terrain" as you are. You can walk, run, or climb almost anywhere.

3 Digesting food

The digestive system (*see page 21*) breaks the banana down into microscopic chemicals that eventually pass into the bloodstream.

4 Feeding the cells

Carried along by your blood, billions of nutritious molecules from the banana are sent where they're most needed – to the billions of cells in every system of your body.

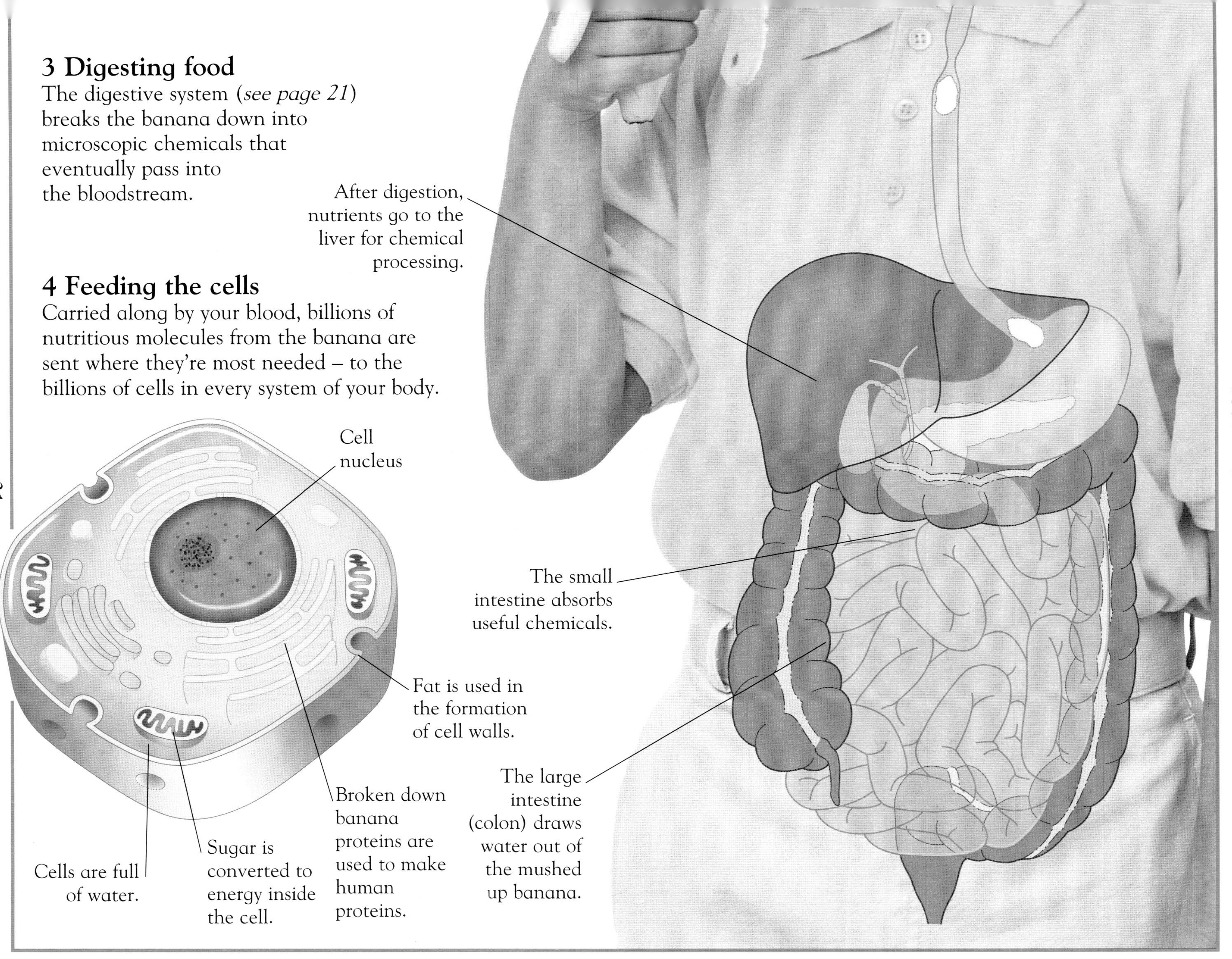

After digestion, nutrients go to the liver for chemical processing.
The small intestine absorbs useful chemicals.
The large intestine (colon) draws water out of the mushed up banana.
Cell nucleus
Fat is used in the formation of cell walls.
Broken down banana proteins are used to make human proteins.
Sugar is converted to energy inside the cell.
Cells are full of water.

The way cells work

Why is the human body like a jail? Because they're both full of cells! (Cells got their name because, long ago, a scientist thought they looked like rows of little rooms.) Each cell has a control center called a nucleus which contains 46 chromosomes. These are made from genetic material called deoxyribonucleic acid, or DNA.

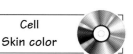

Skin pigment proteins

The cells responsible for the pigment in your skin are called melanocytes. They build the skin-color protein called melanin, which protects you from the Sun. The amount of melanin you have in your skin determines what color your skin is. The more melanin you have, the darker your skin will be.

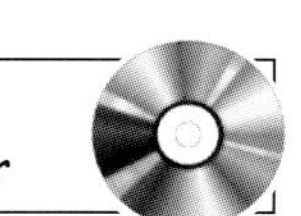
Cell
Skin color

What makes cells look different is the proteins they create.

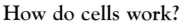

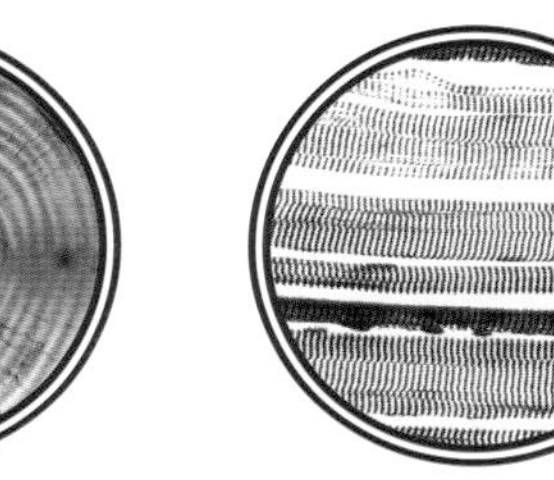
BLOOD CELLS

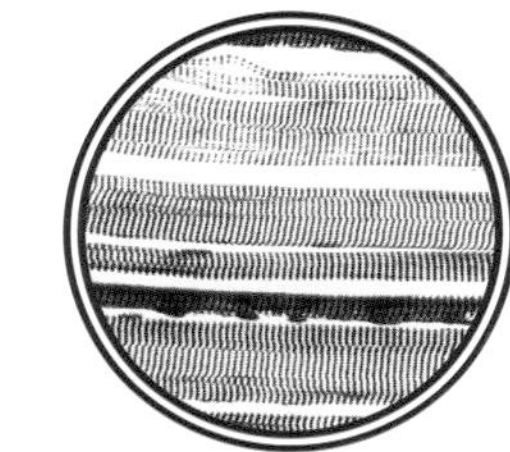
BONE CELLS

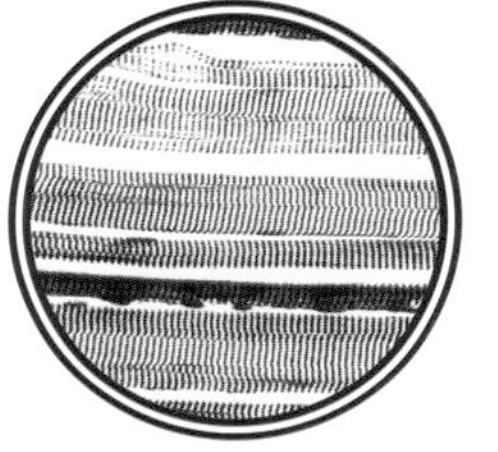
MUSCLE CELLS

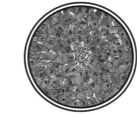

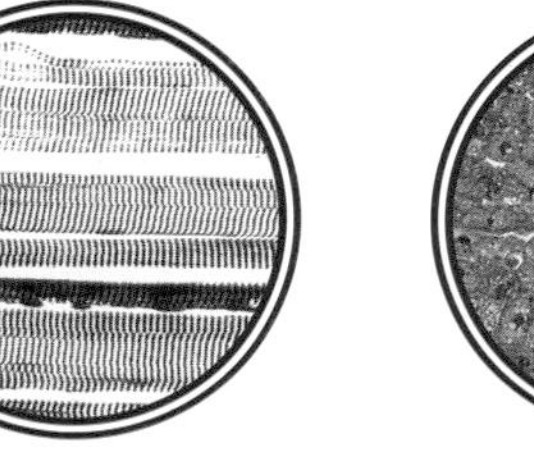
LIVER CELLS

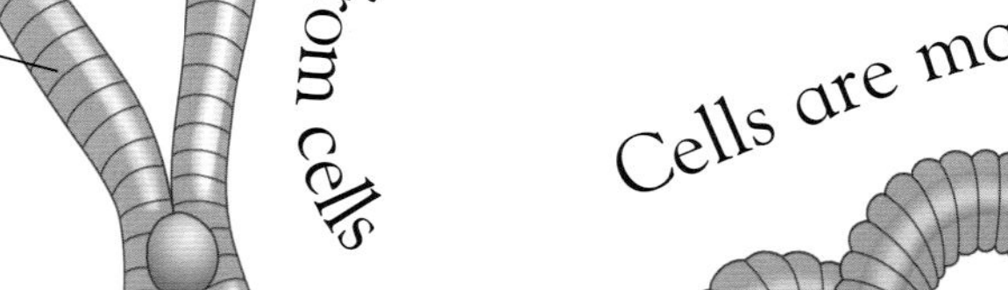
You are made from cells

The cell's nucleus contains the chromosomes.

Each one of the 46 chromosomes inside every cell is made from a single strand of DNA.

How do cells work?

The strands of DNA inside the nucleus of every cell are like a set of recipe books. They hold all the information needed for the thousands of different jobs your body has to do every day to keep you going.

Cells are made from proteins

Genes are the recipes for making protein

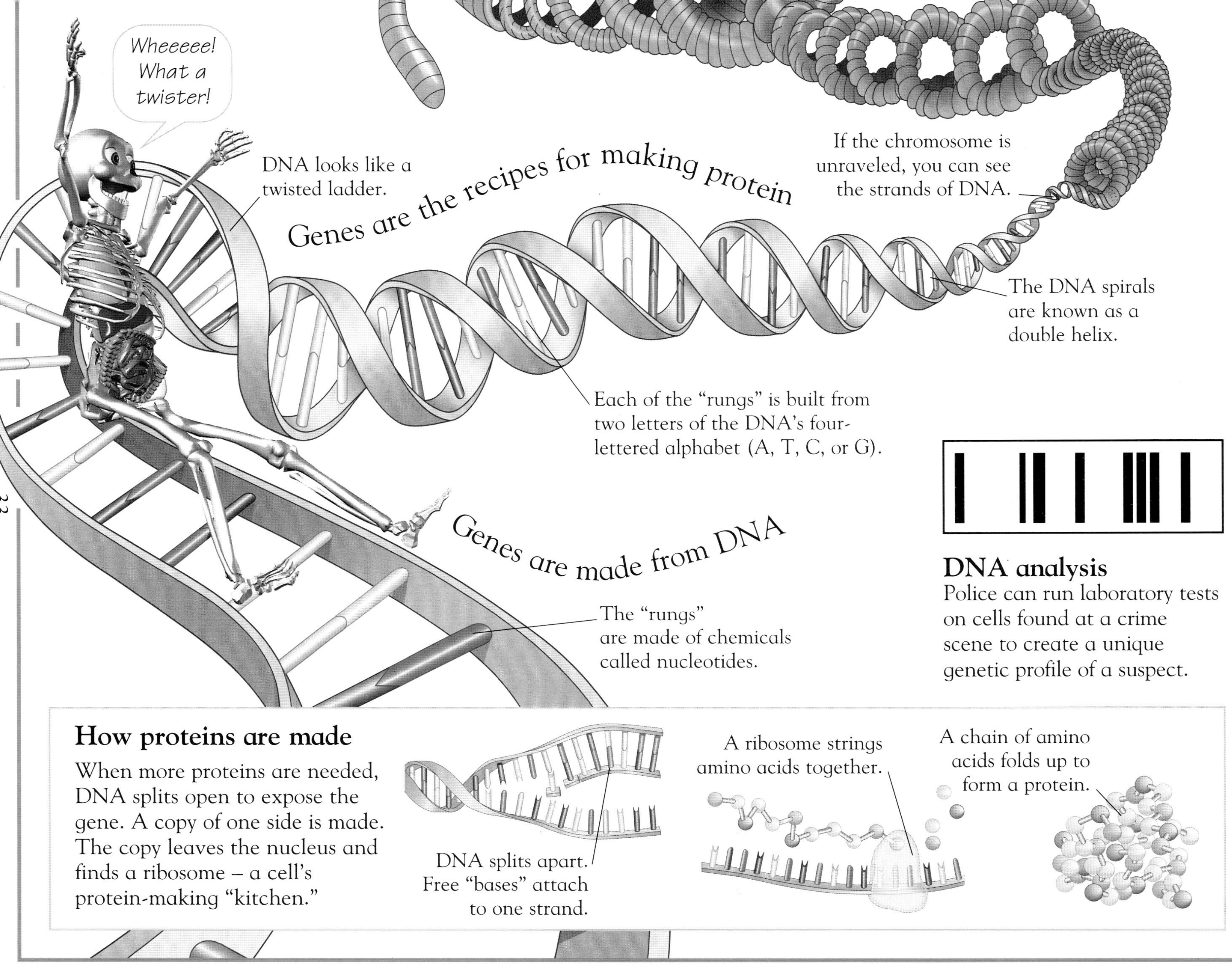

Wheeeee! What a twister!
DNA looks like a twisted ladder.
If the chromosome is unraveled, you can see the strands of DNA.
The DNA spirals are known as a double helix.
Each of the "rungs" is built from two letters of the DNA's four-lettered alphabet (A, T, C, or G).
The "rungs" are made of chemicals called nucleotides.
DNA splits apart. Free "bases" attach to one strand.
A ribosome strings amino acids together.
A chain of amino acids folds up to form a protein.

Genes are made from DNA

DNA analysis

Police can run laboratory tests on cells found at a crime scene to create a unique genetic profile of a suspect.

How proteins are made

When more proteins are needed, DNA splits open to expose the gene. A copy of one side is made. The copy leaves the nucleus and finds a ribosome – a cell's protein-making "kitchen."

Cells make cells

Like all living things, cells eventually die. Your body has an ingenious way of making sure you don't die with them. Thanks to the amazing ability of DNA to make exact copies of itself, the body makes millions of new cells every second to replace the old ones.

Cell copying

Before a cell can divide to make new cells, the DNA inside it has to make a copy of itself. It takes about eight hours to copy all 46 of a cell's chromosomes.

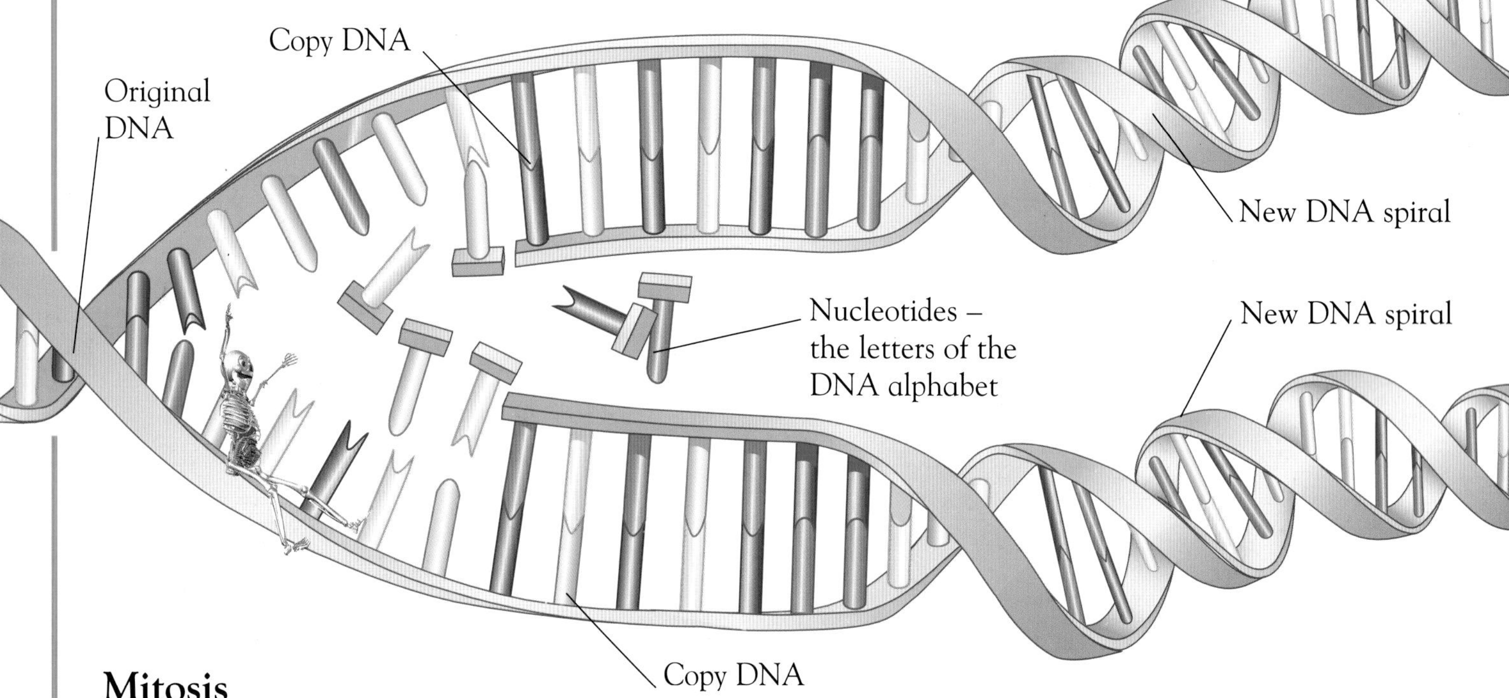

Mitosis

Once the DNA within a cell nucleus has copied itself, the cell can divide to make an identical copy of itself. This process is called mitosis.

Nucleus

ALL 46 CHROMOSOMES ARE DUPLICATED.

Chromosomes line up in the middle of the cell.

METAPHASE

The chromosomes split and each half moves to opposite sides of the cell.

ANAPHASE

A new membrane forms around each of the two new nuclei.

TELOPHASE

The cell has split into two identical cells.

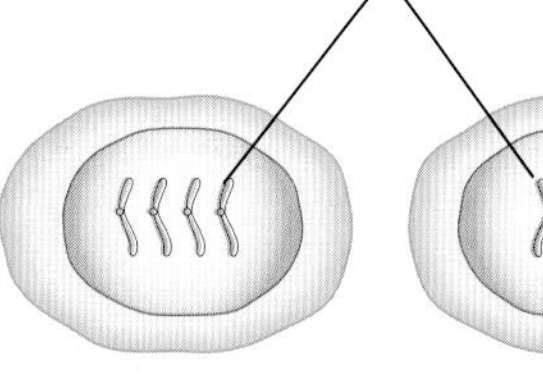

TWO SEPARATE CELLS

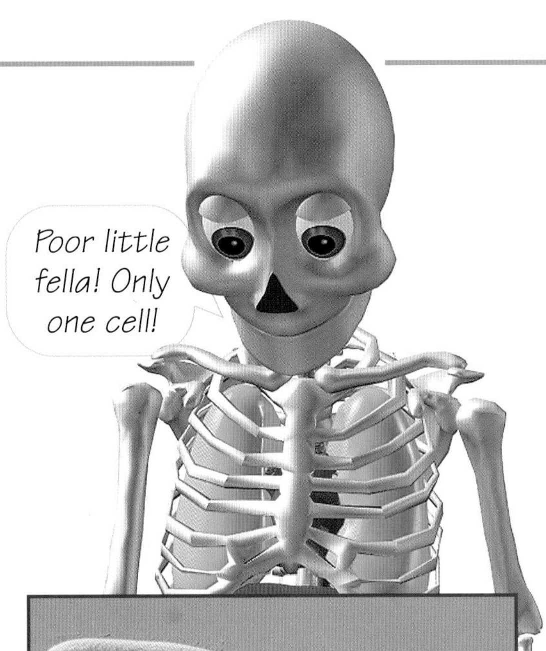
Poor little fella! Only one cell!

Uncontrolled cell growth

A cancer cell is any normal cell that has lost the ability to control its own replication. If cancer cells such as the ones shown here are not stopped by the immune system, they can reproduce uncontrollably and form a growth called a tumor.

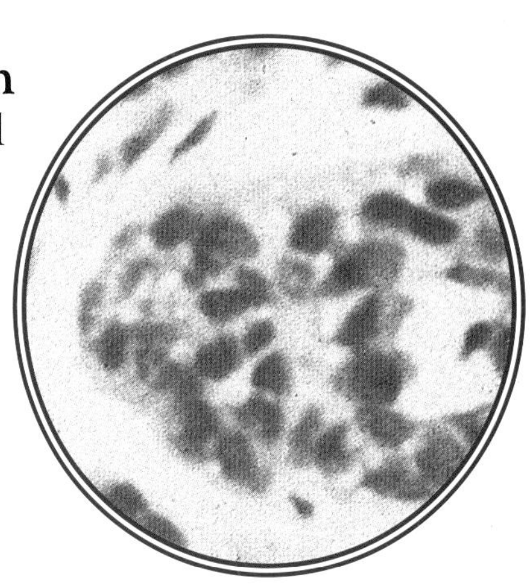

Single-celled animal

Animals such as this paramecium are made of only one cell. They reproduce themselves just like your cells do.

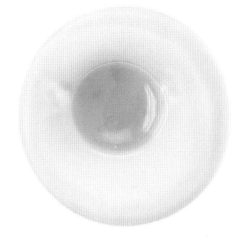

Single cell

Not all cells are minuscule. Did you know that an egg yolk is just one gigantic cell? It's filled with chick-nourishing fats and protein, but contains only one cell nucleus.

Seemore Says

If each of your 50,000 billion cells was as big as a grain of sand, you'd be the size of a very large building! The truth is, you could fit 500 human cells into the period at the end of this sentence.

Moving your body

Movement commands come from different parts of your brain. Voluntary movement is controlled by a part of the brain called the cerebral cortex. Involuntary movement is controlled by the brain stem. The brain sends its commands through a network of nerves – your nervous system.

Ask Seemore

How electric are we?

You have electrical impulses in your nervous system but they are much weaker than even the low-voltage current in a pair of headphones. The voltage in a light bulb is four million times stronger!

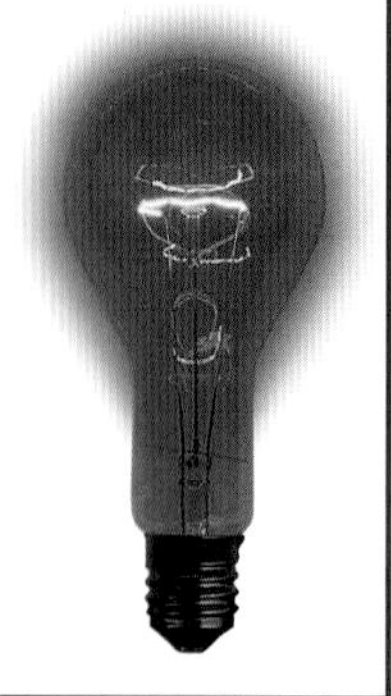

1 Your eyes read the instructions and your brain interprets the words. The message is converted to an electrical impulse.
2 The "move thumb" command starts in the brain's motor command center in the cerebral cortex.
3 The impulse runs down the nerves of the spinal cord like data down a telephone line.
4 The impulse leaves the spinal cord through a gap between two vertebrae and travels down the arm.
One muscle pulls the thumb down. Another muscle pulls it up again.
5 The impulse reaches the thumb-pulling muscles in the hand.

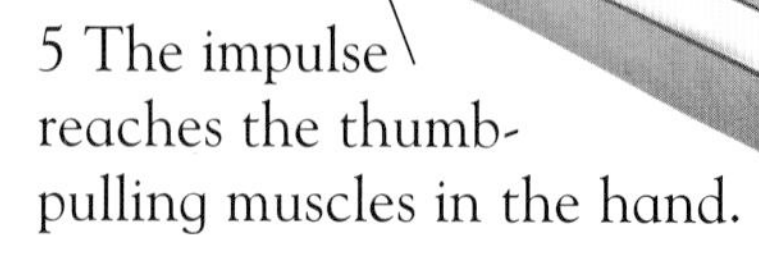

Move a muscle

Ready, get set, flex your thumb! This simple movement actually involves millions of cells and complex chemical reactions. Organs from nearly every system in the body get in on the act.

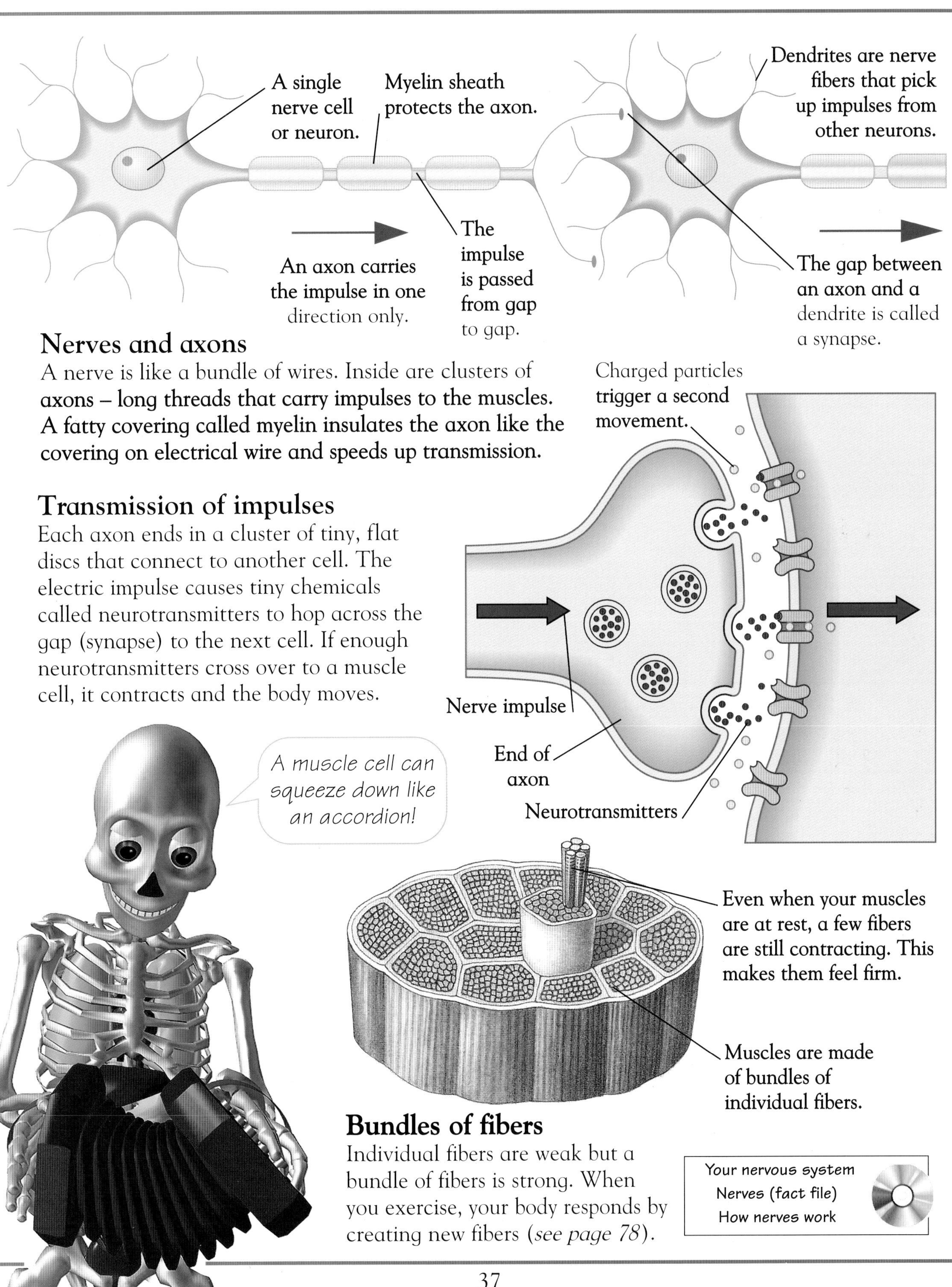

A single nerve cell or neuron.
Myelin sheath protects the axon.
Dendrites are nerve fibers that pick up impulses from other neurons.
An axon carries the impulse in one direction only.
The impulse is passed from gap to gap.
The gap between an axon and a dendrite is called a synapse.
Charged particles trigger a second movement.
Nerve impulse
End of axon
Neurotransmitters
A muscle cell can squeeze down like an accordion!
Even when your muscles are at rest, a few fibers are still contracting. This makes them feel firm.
Muscles are made of bundles of individual fibers.

Nerves and axons

A nerve is like a bundle of wires. Inside are clusters of **axons – long threads that carry impulses to the muscles. A fatty covering called myelin insulates the axon like the covering on electrical wire and speeds up transmission.**

Transmission of impulses

Each axon ends in a cluster of tiny, flat discs that connect to another cell. The electric impulse causes tiny chemicals called neurotransmitters to hop across the gap (synapse) to the next cell. If enough neurotransmitters cross over to a muscle cell, it contracts and the body moves.

Bundles of fibers

Individual fibers are weak but a bundle of fibers is strong. When you exercise, your body responds by creating new fibers (*see page 78*).

Your nervous system
Nerves (fact file)
How nerves work

Make your body go

Why do you breathe? Most importantly, it's because your cells need energy. Without it, they would quickly die. Cells make energy by mixing sugar from the food you eat with oxygen from the air you breathe. Your systems work together to make sure the right organs get the energy they need when they need it. For example, when you ride a bike uphill, your legs need a lot of energy fast.

How does sweat cool the body down? (See page 40)

Seemore Says

Professional cyclists are so fit their hearts pump twice as much blood with each beat as an ordinary person's. At rest, their efficient hearts need only to beat a mere 30 times a minute, compared to around 70 beats a minute for an ordinary person.

Heart rate climbs from 70 to 100 beats per minute.
More blood flows to your legs and buttocks.
Small muscles along your arteries divert blood to your legs.
Your digestive system – Energy

Uphill effort

Riding uphill is hard work for the muscles in your legs and buttocks. They send a chemical message to your brain asking for more sugar and oxygen.

Cheeks redden when blood rushes to the surface in order to release heat into the air.
I've run, and danced, and jumped a lot and now I'm feeling hot, hot, hot!
The lungs continue to pant.
The heartbeat can slowly return to normal.
The legs still need extra oxygen in order to recover from the strain.
TREK

Try it Yourself

Oxygen is needed to release energy. This is true inside the body as well as outside it. You can prove it. Put a tall glass or jar over a lighted candle. After it burns up the oxygen, the flame goes out. Your body also needs a steady supply of oxygen in order to get energy out of the food you eat. You get your oxygen by breathing.

Feel the heat

You need energy to work your muscles. When energy is converted from food to movement, a lot of heat is also generated. When you exercise hard, the heat builds up and has to be released.

Downhill rest

When you ride downhill, your body can recover from the stresses and strains of the climb. It also takes the chance to build up a few more proteins so that you'll be better prepared the next time you reach a big hill.

Chemical balance

It may be cold and windy outside, but inside your skin the weather is always the same – warm and wet. It's like a swamp in there! When it comes to temperature, water balance, and chemical content, your body is very particular about the way things should be.

Sweat is secreted by the sweat glands.

SWEAT

Tiny muscles make hairs stand up to trap warm air.

GOOSE PIMPLES

Heat out

Your skin uses sweat to help maintain your temperature. When sweat evaporates, it draws surplus heat away from your body to cool you down.

Heat in

When it's cold, you shiver and get goose pimples. Less blood flows to the body's surface, which helps to conserve the warmth of your organs deep inside.

Cold- and warm-blooded

Cold-blooded lizards have to bask in the sun to reach their optimal temperature. Humans are warm-blooded which means our bodies are kept at 98° F (37° C) no matter what the weather.

Ask Seemore

Why does sweat smell?

It doesn't. But the bacteria that eat the special fats in sweat excrete a very strong-smelling chemical. Your sweat glands don't produce these fats until you've reached puberty.

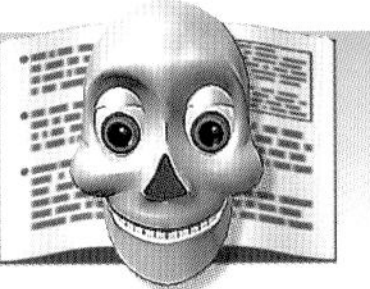

Seemore Says

People who drink a lot of alcohol can damage their liver. Cirrhosis is a disease caused by too much alcohol. Sometimes, the damage never heals and the disease is fatal.

Body chemistry

The human body is one big chemistry set. It relies on having the right balance of chemicals around in order to do all its jobs, from building cells to flexing muscles. That's why we have the most incredible chemical treatment plant inside our bodies. It's the liver!

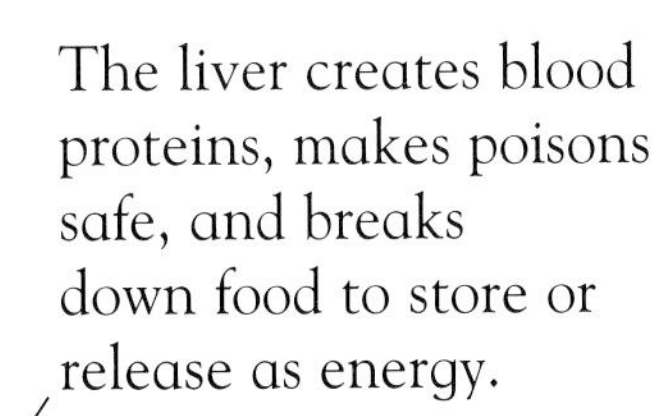

The liver creates blood proteins, makes poisons safe, and breaks down food to store or release as energy.

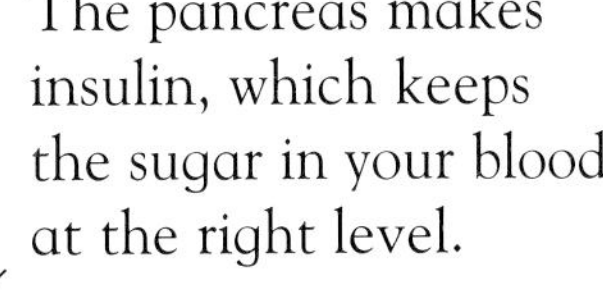

The pancreas makes insulin, which keeps the sugar in your blood at the right level.

Kidneys adjust the concentration of urine to maintain water balance.

Water level

To keep the cells working and your blood flowing easily, your body does its best to keep water content at around 62% of your body weight.

Inside your skin Sweat glands
Hair muscle Feeling hot
Feeling cold Liver fact file

How to fight germs

Once a virus or harmful bacterium gets inside you, it tries to form a huge colony that can make you sick. From the wax in your ears to the mucus in your nose, your body has a range of ways to keep germs out. If germs *do* get in, it's up to the white blood cells (lymphocytes) to swing into action. White blood cells remember each germ so that they can fight it more quickly if it makes a second attack.

Bacteria
Bacteria are single-celled animals. Some are very useful to your body, but others make you feel ill.

The front line

Skin creates a near-perfect barrier against germs. Unfortunately, skin has "holes" in it, so your body has guards posted at all the openings to keep germ invaders away.

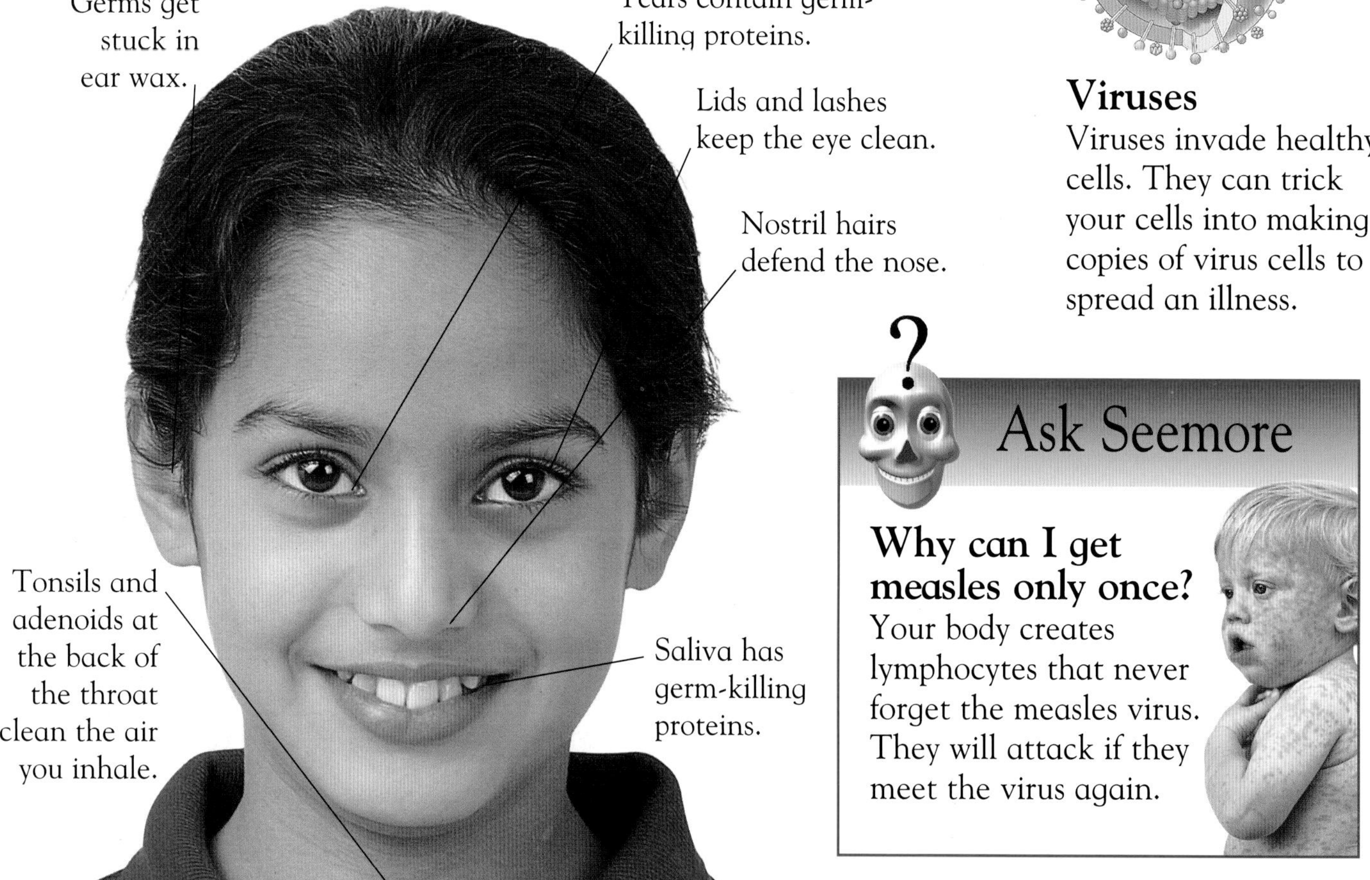
Germs get stuck in ear wax.
Tears contain germ-killing proteins.
Lids and lashes keep the eye clean.
Nostril hairs defend the nose.
Tonsils and adenoids at the back of the throat clean the air you inhale.
Saliva has germ-killing proteins.

Viruses
Viruses invade healthy cells. They can trick your cells into making copies of virus cells to spread an illness.

Ask Seemore

Why can I get measles only once?
Your body creates lymphocytes that never forget the measles virus. They will attack if they meet the virus again.

Bacteria bashing

Made in the bone marrow, lymph nodes, and the spleen, lymphocytes search for bacteria to destroy.

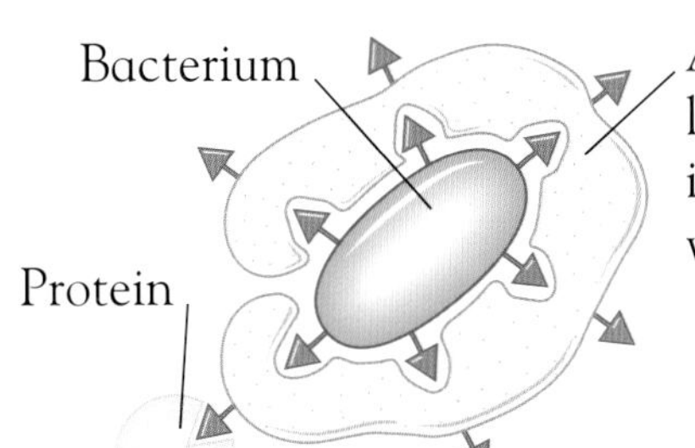

1 A lymphocyte "learns" to recognize an enemy bacterium

2 The lymphocyte builds antibodies to use in the war against bacterial invaders.

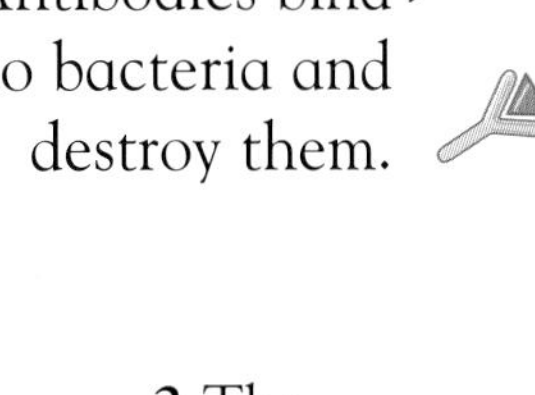

3 Antibodies bind to bacteria and destroy them.

More cells arrive to assist in the battle.

Victory over viruses

How do you identify your enemy if you don't have eyes to see them? Lymphocytes are chemical police officers. They check their suspects for tell-tale proteins.

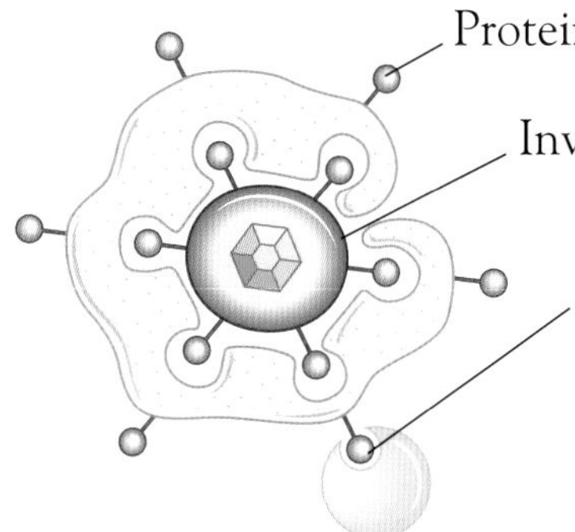

1 The lymphocyte "shows" a virus protein to another kind of lymphocyte called a T-cell.

2 The T-cells reproduce to make killer cells full of antibodies.

3 Killer cells bombard viruses with antibodies.

Killer cells develop and mature in the thymus.

Lymph nodes are home to millions of white blood cells.

Lymph vessels carry lymph to every cell in your body.

Lymphocytes mature in the spleen.

Lymphatic system

Lymph is a fluid filled with germ-killing lymphocytes. It travels through a network of lymph vessels. The bumps along the major vessels are called lymph nodes. When your body is fighting off an infection, your lymph nodes may swell up.

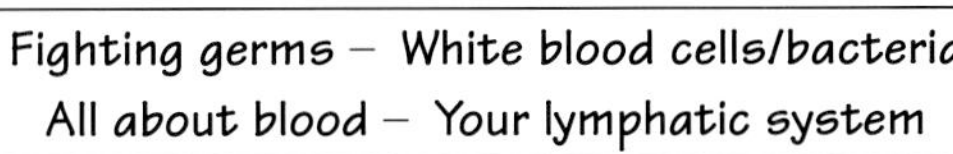

Fighting germs – White blood cells/bacteria
All about blood – Your lymphatic system

Mend a broken body

Our bodies come complete with their very own repair kits. Everything you need to patch up all but the most severe injuries is right there in your blood. Whenever you get a cut, scrape, or broken bone, these repair-kit cells will be on the job faster than you can say "Seemore Skinless"!

Keep still! Help is on the way!

How scabs form

When a blood vessel is cut, platelets in the blood race to the rescue. They produce a chemical that slows down blood flow. Fibrin strands, formed by a protein in the blood, form a mesh, or scab, to plug the hole.

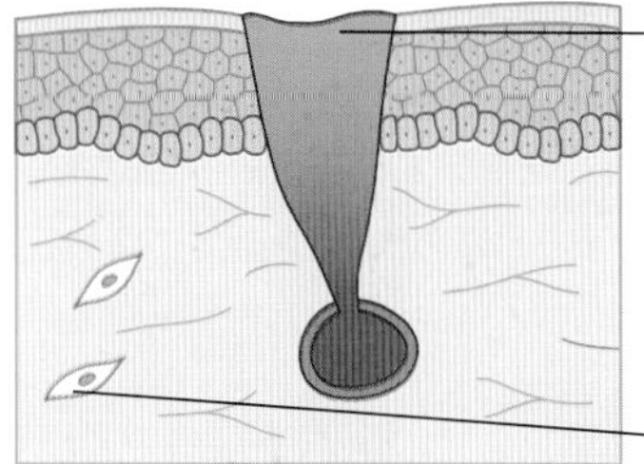

Fibrin traps red blood cells and starts to form a clot.

White blood cells rush to the scene.

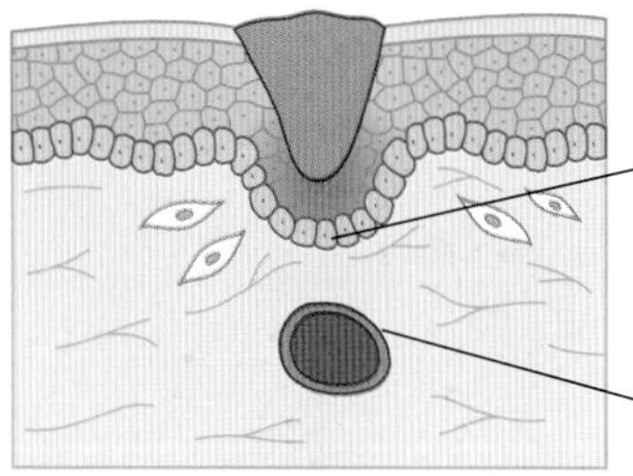

Skin cells reach out to one another across the gap.

The blood vessel repairs its own puncture.

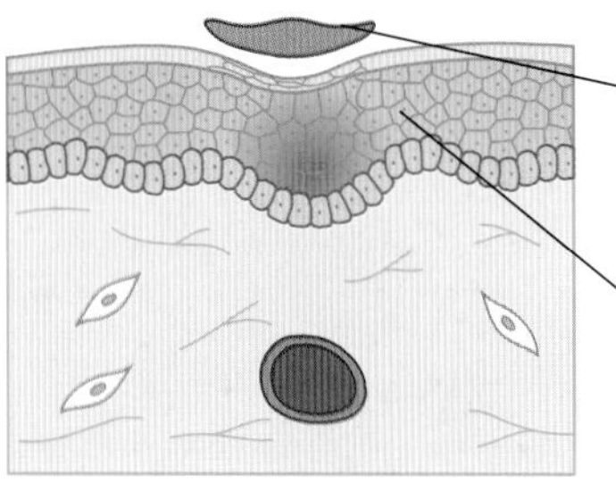

The scab falls away when the skin cells beneath it mature and die.

New skin cells multiply quickly to create a thick barrier.

Injured knee

Cuts, scrapes, and breaks in the skin provide germs with a new way in to your body. If your injury becomes infected, it will feel warm, look red, and hurt! Antiseptic cream can help your immune system fight off the germs.

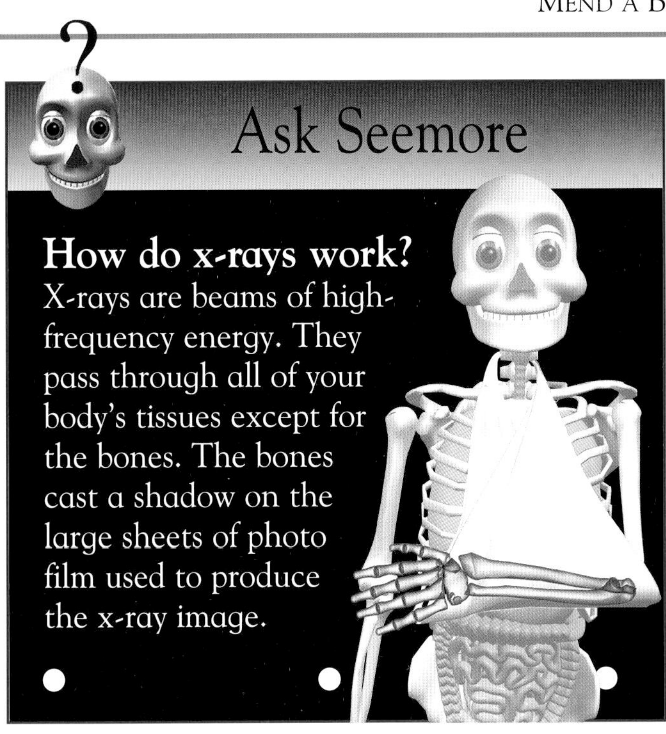

Ask Seemore

How do x-rays work?
X-rays are beams of high-frequency energy. They pass through all of your body's tissues except for the bones. The bones cast a shadow on the large sheets of photo film used to produce the x-ray image.

How cuts heal X-rays
Broken bones

Mending bones
Although they're incredibly strong and flexible, even bones break when the strain is too great. But because they're made by living cells, they can repair themselves.

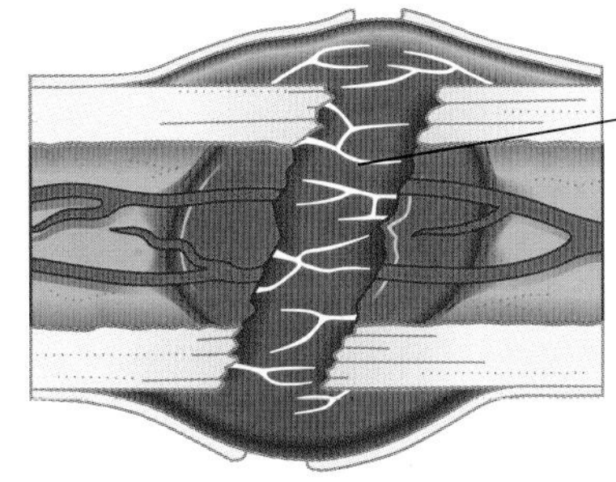

After the break, protein ropes form a scaffolding for the healing cartilage and bone-making cells.

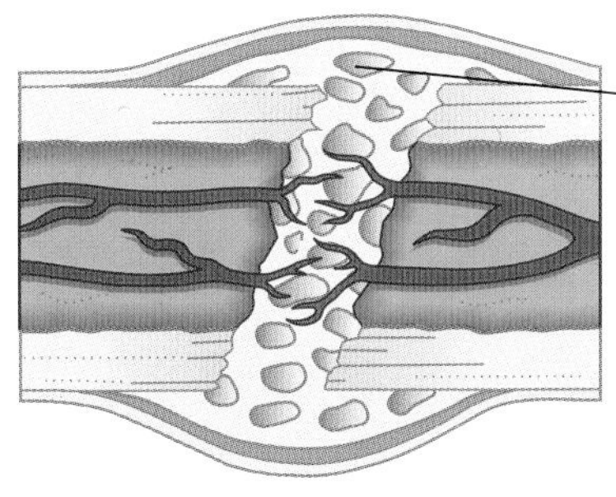

Bone-builders (osteoblasts) lay on new bone thickly, leaving a very chunky repair patch.

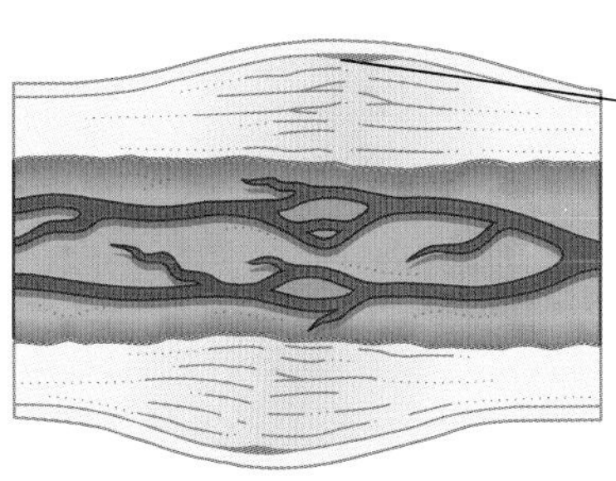

Osteoclasts (bone breakers) eat away excess bone and make the patch tidy.

How should you treat a cut? (See page 90)

In stitches
When a cut is too wide and deep for a scab to form, you need stitches to hold the skin in place while the cut heals.

How you think

With every thought, an electrical current spreads through the brain's intricate web of connections. Some of it is under your control – that's your conscious thought. But much more thought goes on without you knowing about it. This mixture of feelings, fears, and beliefs is known as your subconscious.

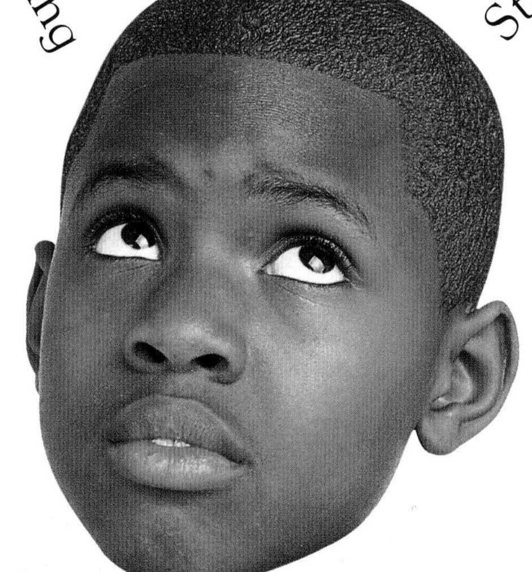

How do nerve cells work? (See page 37)

Think about it!

From daydreaming to memorizing spellings, all thought is caused by electrical current flowing along neuron pathways through the regions of your brain. Mental activities such as reading and puzzles build connections and help your brain to work faster.

Try it Yourself

The way we think depends on who we are. Try this yourself, then ask friends or members of your family the same question. Look at the glass and describe what you see. Is the glass half full or half empty? There is a belief that saying it's "half full" reveals an optimistic outlook, while saying it's "half empty" means a negative outlook.

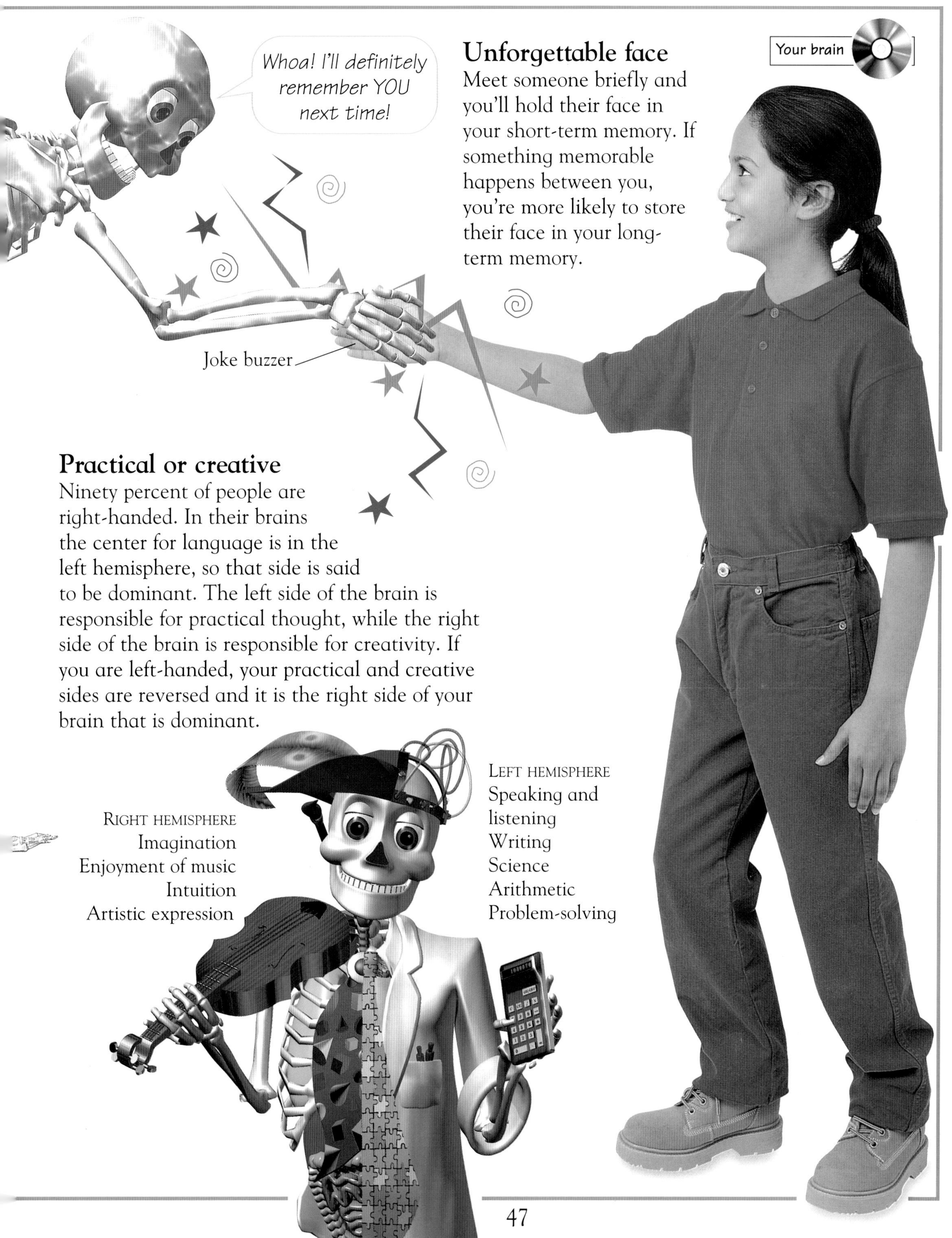

Unforgettable face

Meet someone briefly and you'll hold their face in your short-term memory. If something memorable happens between you, you're more likely to store their face in your long-term memory.

Practical or creative

Ninety percent of people are right-handed. In their brains the center for language is in the left hemisphere, so that side is said to be dominant. The left side of the brain is responsible for practical thought, while the right side of the brain is responsible for creativity. If you are left-handed, your practical and creative sides are reversed and it is the right side of your brain that is dominant.

Communicating

What good is it having a big brain if you can't tell someone else what you're thinking? Most human beings are naturally sociable, and every human community has developed its own language. But we also send out a whole range of silent messages – often without our knowledge – that can speak even louder than words.

HAPPY

ANGRY

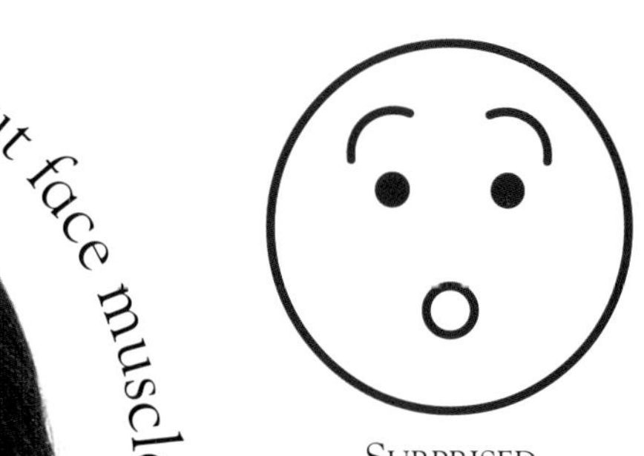

SURPRISED

SAD

Communication center

Four of your five senses are based in your head. The head is the beacon from which you send messages out to the world, and the antenna by which you receive communication from others (*see page 25*).

What is special about face muscles? (*See page 13*)

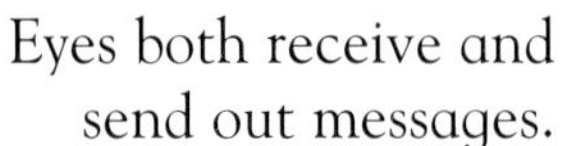

Eyes both receive and send out messages.

You receive information through your nose too.

Eyes and ears are signal receivers.

Tongue taps, clicks, and trills.

Lips change the shape of the mouth.

Vibrating vocal cords make sound.

Browbeaten

Your eyebrows help to communicate your emotions. Even on a simple drawing, rearranging the eyebrows' position gives a face a different attitude.

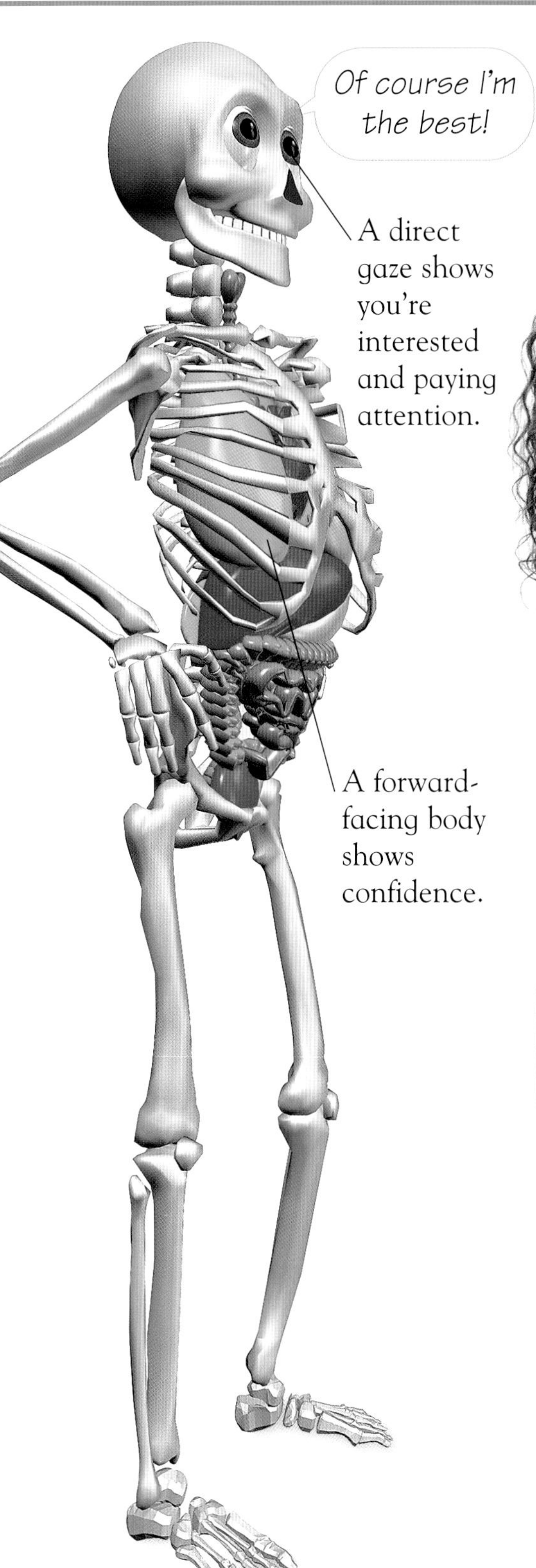

Of course I'm the best!
A direct gaze shows you're interested and paying attention.
A forward-facing body shows confidence.
Looking or turning away shows you are not interested or paying attention.
Crossing your arms shows that you feel defensive.

How your voice works
Vocal cords

Keeping in touch

Ten innovations devised by humans to improve human communication.

1 The alphabet
2 Paper
3 The printing press
4 Morse code
5 The telephone
6 The tape recorder
7 Radio
8 Television
9 Communication satellites
10 The Internet

Seemore Says

Many animals communicate through the language of smells. Humans do too, and we send out subtle messages to attract a mate. People often use soap to keep odors at bay, but some perfumes are actually made from the same secretions animals use to attract a mate.

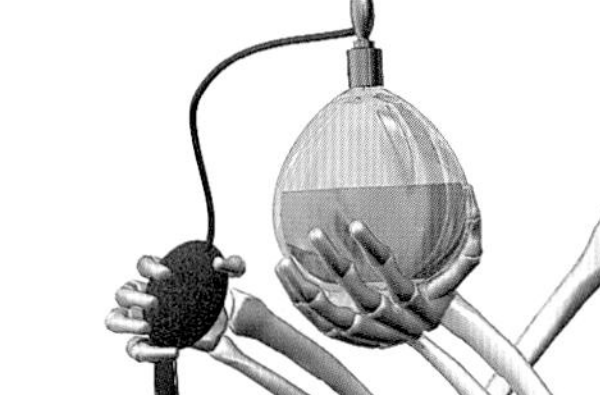

Body language

There are many ways to say something other than with speech. Our body language can say "I want it my way," or we might shield our bodies when we feel insecure, or use touch as a sign of friendship and trust.

Growing-up guide

Mountains are millions of years old and stars are billions of years old. Compared to them, a human lifetime passes in an instant. A human life is like a story. It has a beginning, a middle, and an end. Our job is to make our lives as interesting and rewarding as possible, and to put off the end for as long as we can!

This section takes you through the whole human life cycle, from the beginning of life as a tiny embryo, to the choices you make as a teenager, and, finally, the changes that every human body goes through as it gets older.

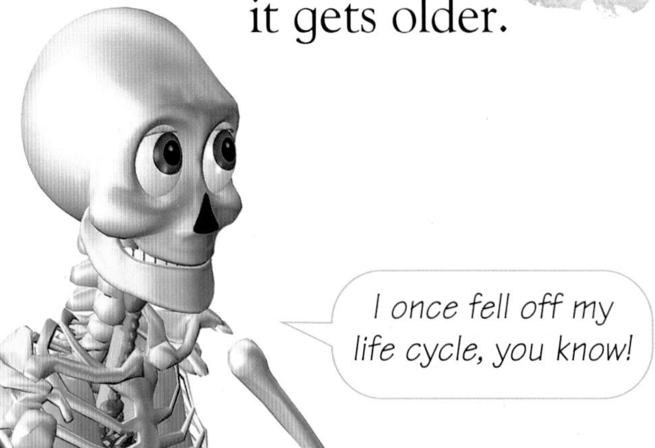

I once fell off my life cycle, you know!

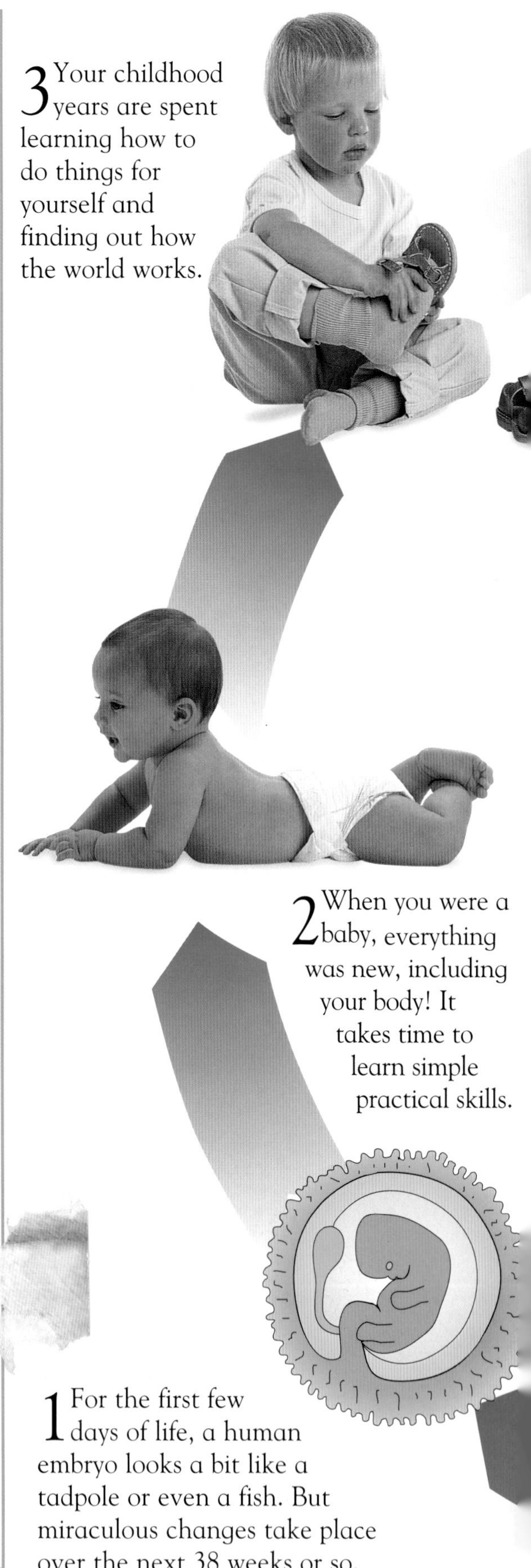

3 Your childhood years are spent learning how to do things for yourself and finding out how the world works.

2 When you were a baby, everything was new, including your body! It takes time to learn simple practical skills.

1 For the first few days of life, a human embryo looks a bit like a tadpole or even a fish. But miraculous changes take place over the next 38 weeks or so.

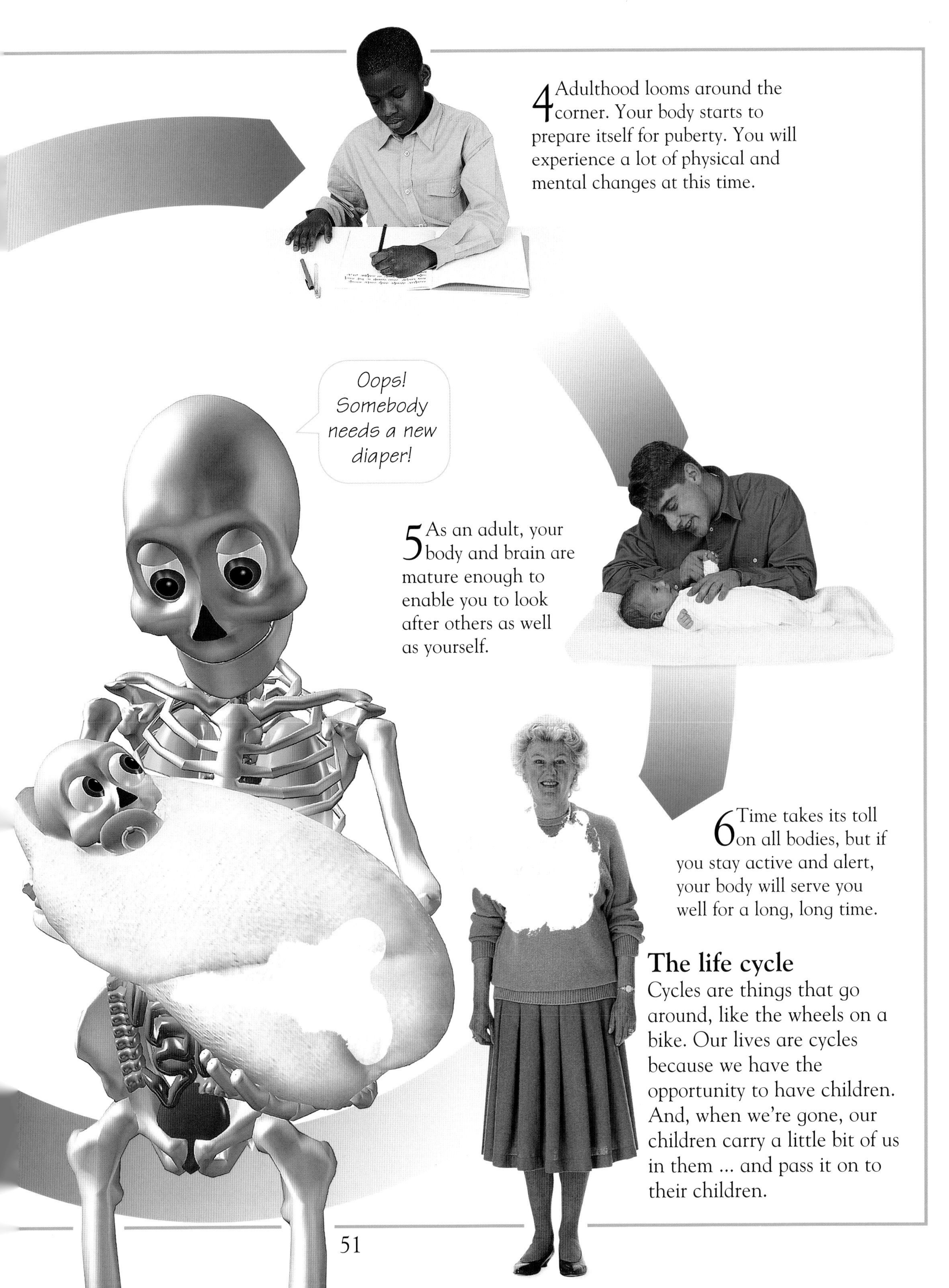
Oops!
Somebody
needs a new
diaper!

4 Adulthood looms around the corner. Your body starts to prepare itself for puberty. You will experience a lot of physical and mental changes at this time.

5 As an adult, your body and brain are mature enough to enable you to look after others as well as yourself.

6 Time takes its toll on all bodies, but if you stay active and alert, your body will serve you well for a long, long time.

The life cycle

Cycles are things that go around, like the wheels on a bike. Our lives are cycles because we have the opportunity to have children. And, when we're gone, our children carry a little bit of us in them ... and pass it on to their children.

Great genes

Aaaagh! He looks just like me!

Each of your genes contains a characteristic, such as eye colour or hair type, that is inherited from your parents and grandparents. Because of the mix-and-match way your genes were put together, you can truthfully say that you were built from a set of genes that no-one has ever had before (unless you're an identical twin).

What are genes made from? (See pages 32–33)

Which genes?

Your mother and father gave you genes that conflicted with one another. Your body decided which instructions to follow according to certain rules. For example, the gene for brown eyes is always "dominant", which means it will overrule a "recessive" blue eyes gene. Other traits, such as hair type, are usually a mixture of several genes from both parents.

Pick a toy

Boys and girls tend to show different interests even at a young age. Some scientists say that genes give girls and boys different interests. Others believe that children are influenced more by the people around them. Really, both factors are at work.

How twins form

One in three twin births produces identical twins. They form when the developing embryo splits to make two babies with exactly the same genes. Fraternal (non-identical) twins form when two eggs are released by the mother and each is fertilised by a separate sperm.

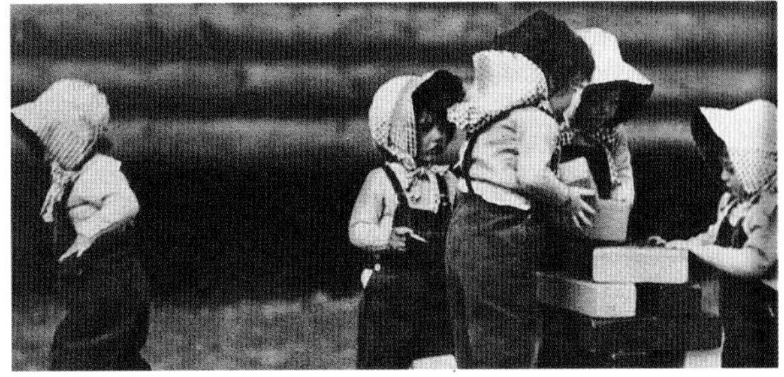

Quintuplets

Sometimes, several babies develop in the womb. The first known quintuplets (five babies born at once) to survive into adulthood were the Dionnes, born in Canada in 1934. Multiple births usually come from separate eggs. The Dionnes, however, were a very rare occurrence of identical quintuplets from just one egg.

"Siamese" twins

Very rarely, an embryo splits later in the pregnancy but does not separate completely. This produces twins who share one or more body parts. A famous pair were brothers Chang and Eng from Siam (now Thailand).

Seemore Says

Fingerprints are unique, so not even identical twins have the same ones. We have a different fingerprint on each finger. The most common type is the loop. Whorls are also quite common, but only 15% of people have the arch fingerprint.

ARCH

LOOP

WHORL

COMPOSITE

Skin and touching
Your fingerprints

Egg meets sperm

One day, about nine months before you were born, you were conceived. One of your father's sperm entered your mother's fertile egg and something miraculous happened. Fifty thousand of your father's genes met up with fifty thousand of your mother's genes. They formed a cell with a unique set of genetic instructions – half his and half hers. Following those instructions, that cell divided and grew to form you.

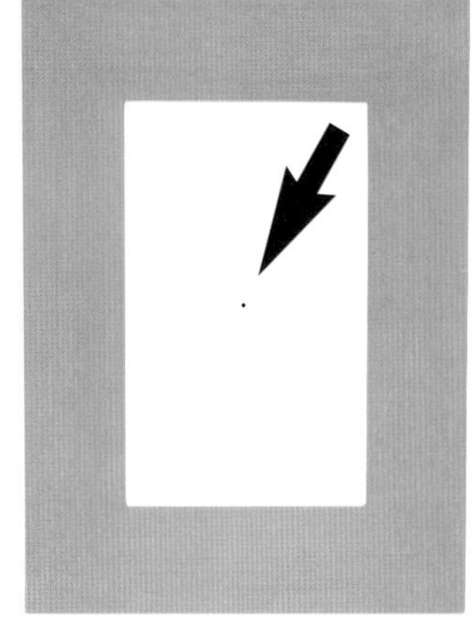

The egg
Humans come from tiny beginnings. Can you believe you were once this small?

How do the sperm and the egg get together in the first place? (See page 27)

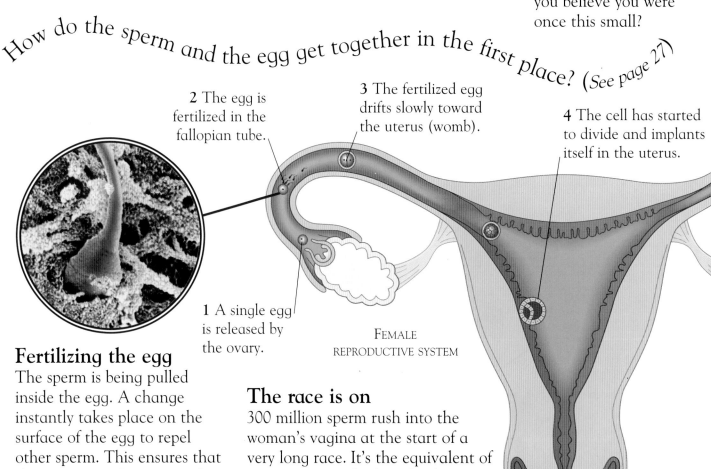

2 The egg is fertilized in the fallopian tube.

3 The fertilized egg drifts slowly toward the uterus (womb).

4 The cell has started to divide and implants itself in the uterus.

1 A single egg is released by the ovary.

FEMALE REPRODUCTIVE SYSTEM

Fertilizing the egg
The sperm is being pulled inside the egg. A change instantly takes place on the surface of the egg to repel other sperm. This ensures that the egg gets only one set of the father's chromosomes.

The race is on
300 million sperm rush into the woman's vagina at the start of a very long race. It's the equivalent of you swimming the length of more than 90 Olympic swimming pools.

Gene swapping

Pairs of chromosomes, like the two below, often swap genes. This process only happens in the creation of sperm and eggs and shuffles the genes around before they are used in the design of a new baby.

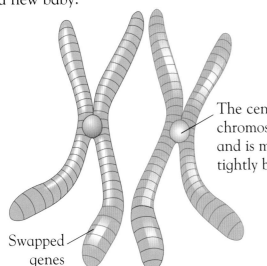

The centromere is the chromosome's "handle" and is made from tightly bundled DNA.

Swapped genes

Ask Seemore

Brother or sister?

Eggs always carry the X chromosome, which has only female traits. Sperm may carry either the X or the male Y chromosome. This means that the sex of a baby is always determined by the father.

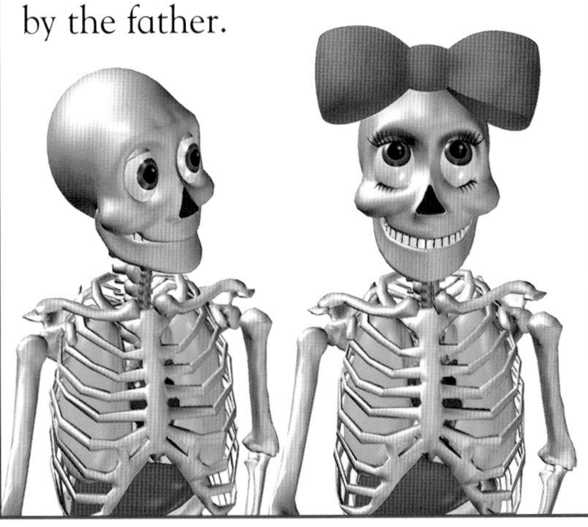

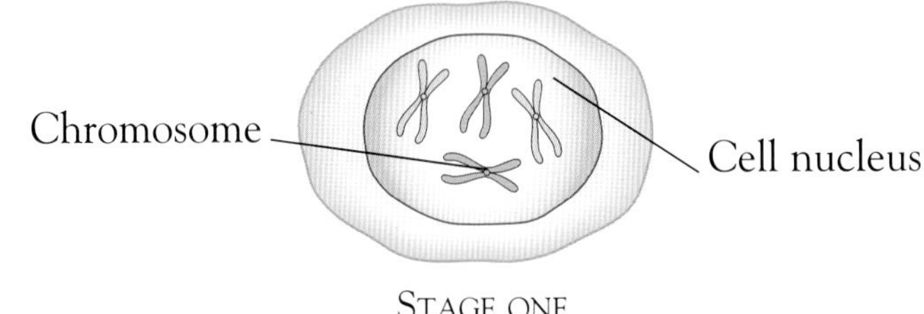

Chromosome
Cell nucleus

Stage one

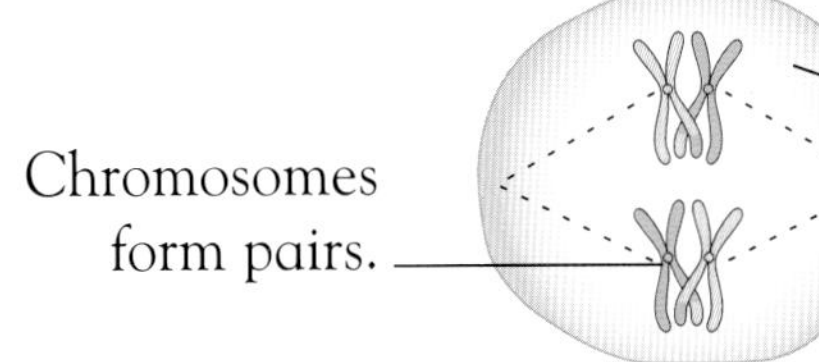

Chromosomes form pairs.
The nucleus membrane disappears.

Stage two

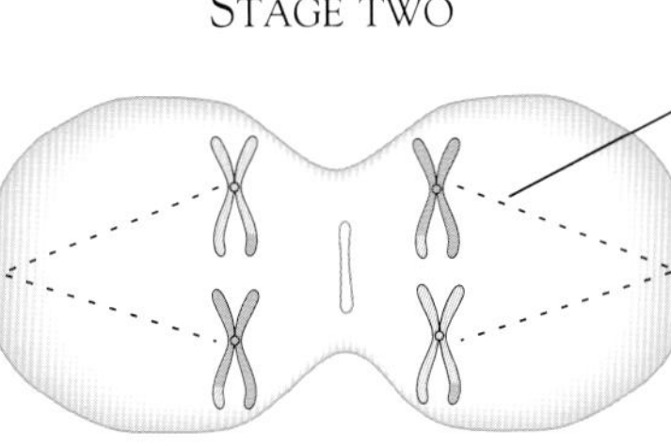

Threads form and pull the chromosomes apart.

Stage three

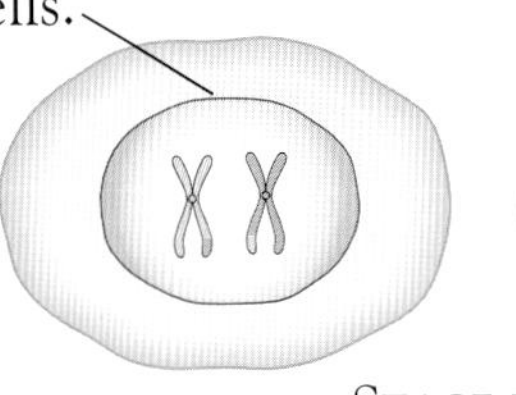
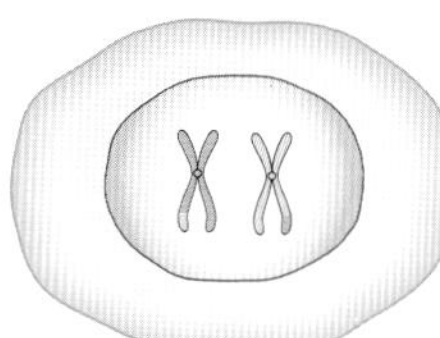

The cell divides into two new cells.

Stage four

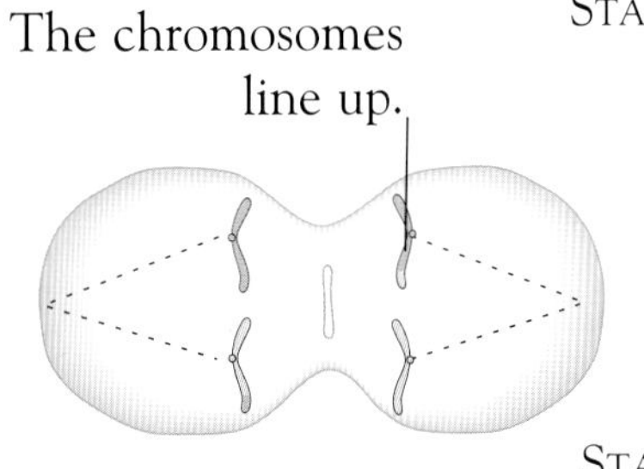
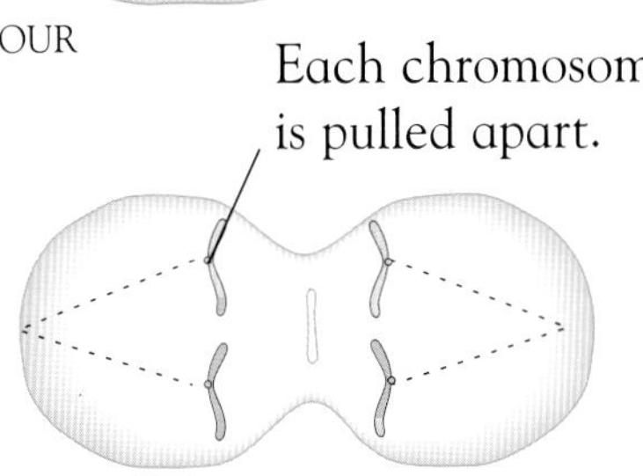

The chromosomes line up.
Each chromosome is pulled apart.

Stage five

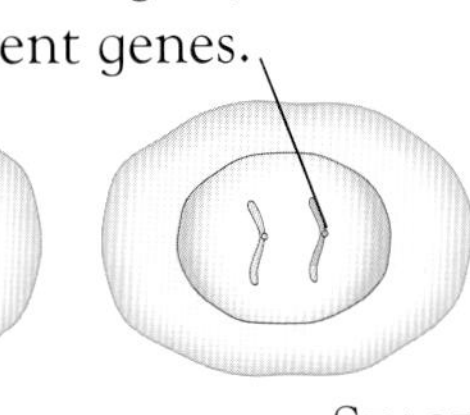
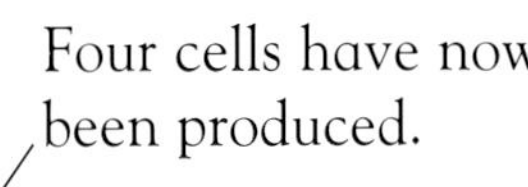
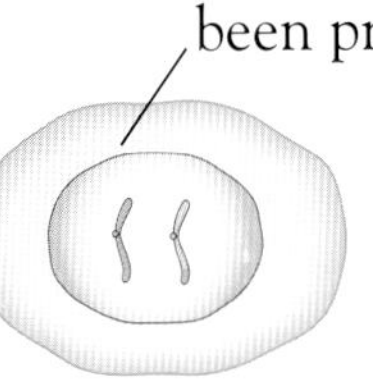
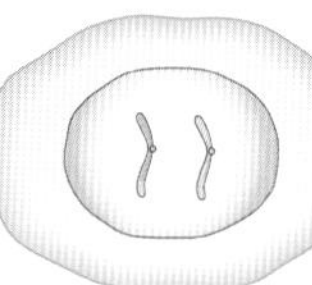

Each cell has slightly different genes.
Four cells have now been produced.

Stage six

Meiosis

Most cells have 46 chromosomes (23 pairs) – 23 from your mother and 23 from your father. But the baby-making sex cells – egg and sperm – have only half a set. Both are created in the same process called meiosis. For simplicity, only four chromosomes are shown here.

In the womb

Humans are mammals, which means that our young are protected inside their mothers' bodies at the start of their lives. The mother's body makes a placenta, a disk-shaped organ that transfers oxygen and nutrients to the growing baby. The baby is attached to the placenta via the umbilical cord. This acts as a feeding and breathing tube until the baby is born.

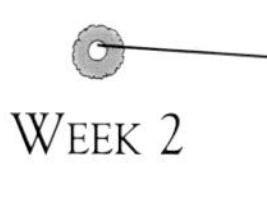

The cluster of cells forms an embryo.

Week 2

The cells start to form a tube shape.

Week 3

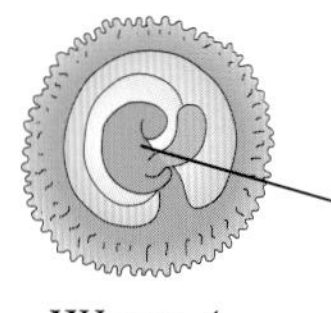

A heart forms and starts to beat.

Week 4

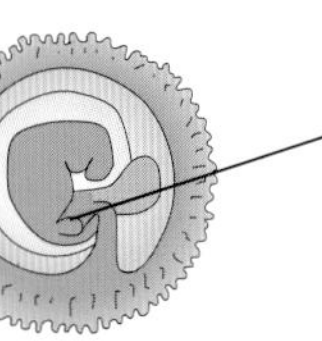

Hands appear and the digestive system forms.

Week 5

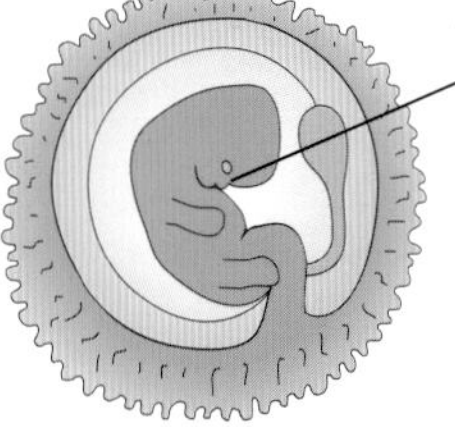

Nose and eyelids appear and the skeleton is formed.

Week 6

Settling in

It takes the whole of the first week for the fertilized egg to make the 4 in (10 cm) journey down the fallopian tube and into the uterus. The cells go through several divisions and yet, at the end of week two, the whole cluster of cells is barely bigger than the egg it first came from.

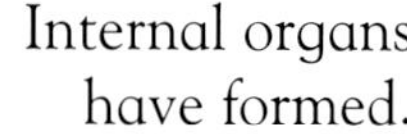
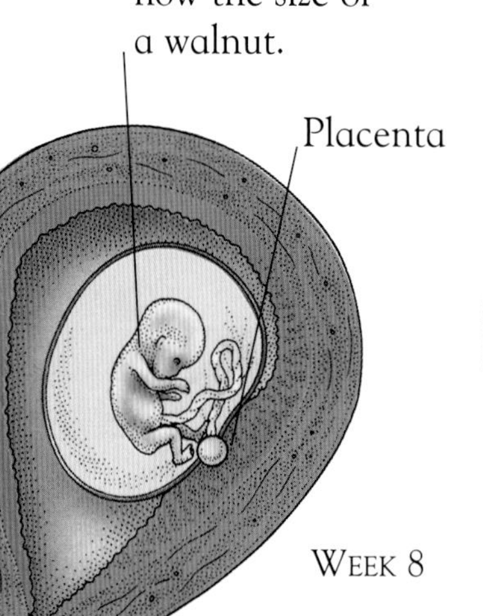

The embryo is now the size of a walnut.
Placenta

Week 8

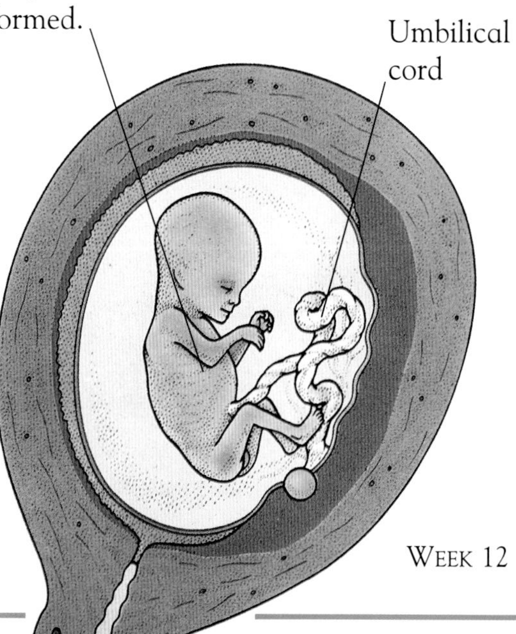

Internal organs have formed.
Umbilical cord

Week 12

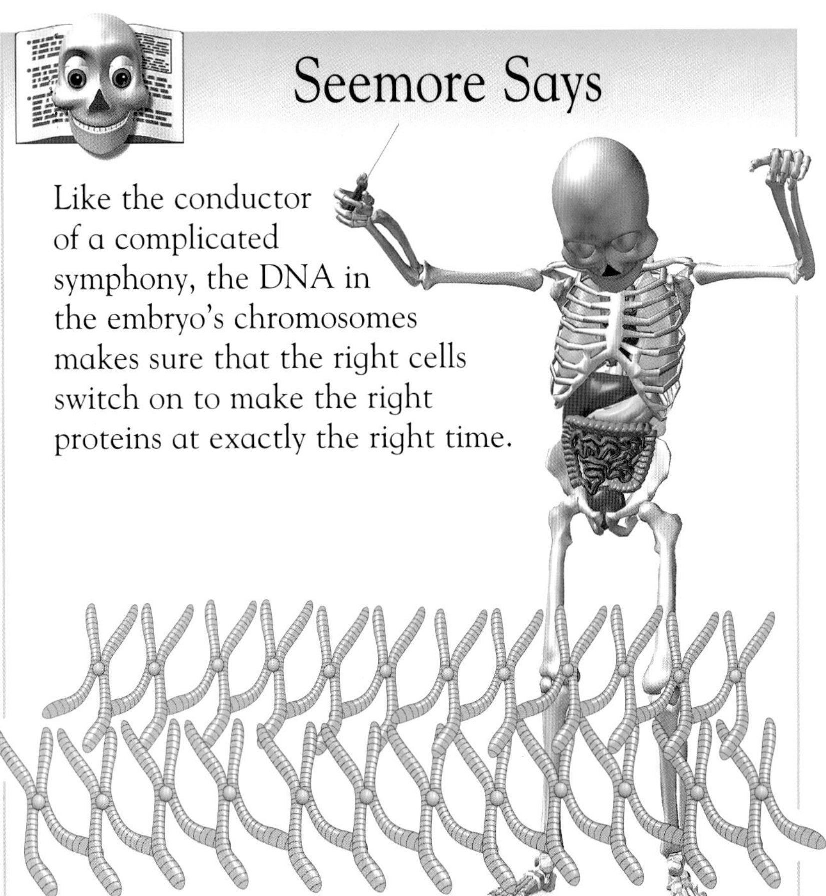

Seemore Says

Like the conductor of a complicated symphony, the DNA in the embryo's chromosomes makes sure that the right cells switch on to make the right proteins at exactly the right time.

Growing and changing
Where babies come from

Getting ready to be born

Premature babies born as early as 24 weeks have a chance of surviving outside the womb. However, most stay in for an average of 38 weeks. During the final weeks of development, the baby puts on fat to fuel it through the trauma of being born. It practices its breathing movements and becomes sensitive to the light. The baby's head drops down into the mother's pelvis in preparation for its entrance into the outside world.

What happens if the egg isn't fertilized? (See page 64)

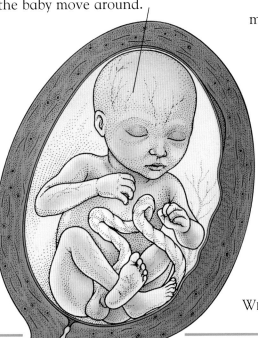

The fetus continues to grow. The mother starts to feel the baby move around.

WEEK 16

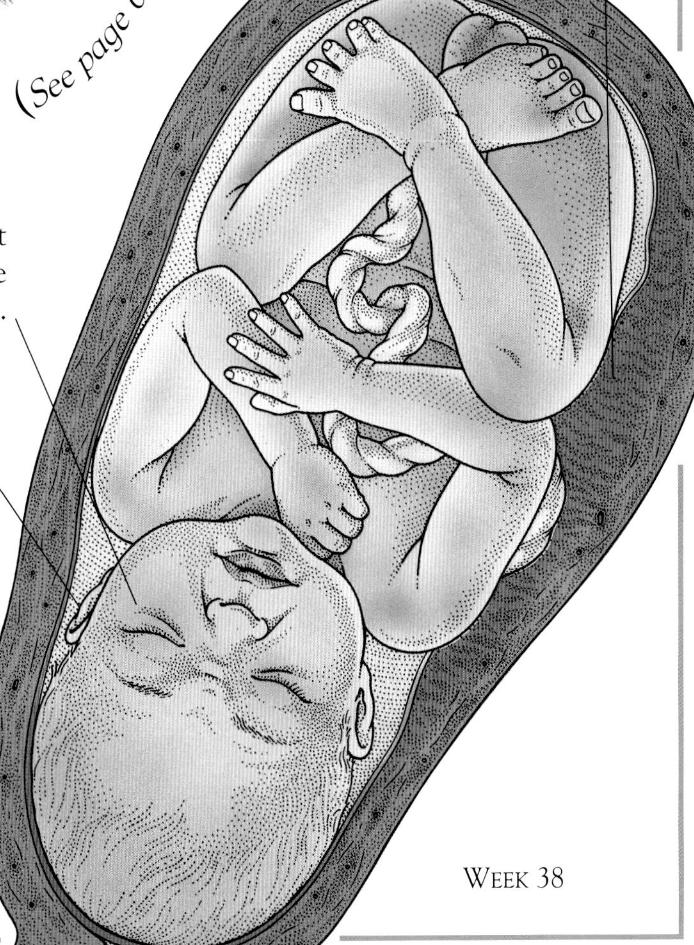

The placenta will detach itself during the birth.

Eyes can see light shining on the mother's tummy.

Ears can hear the mother's heartbeat.

WEEK 38

A new life

When the time is right, strong muscle spasms, called contractions, open the mother's uterus so the baby can come out. The placenta detaches itself and follows. The umbilical cord must be cut and clamped. Later, it will wither away and leave just a navel – a souvenir from nine months in the womb that you will have for the rest of your life.

Baby bonding
In the first few hours of life, most newborn babies and their parents form a strong bond – the beginning of a lifelong relationship.

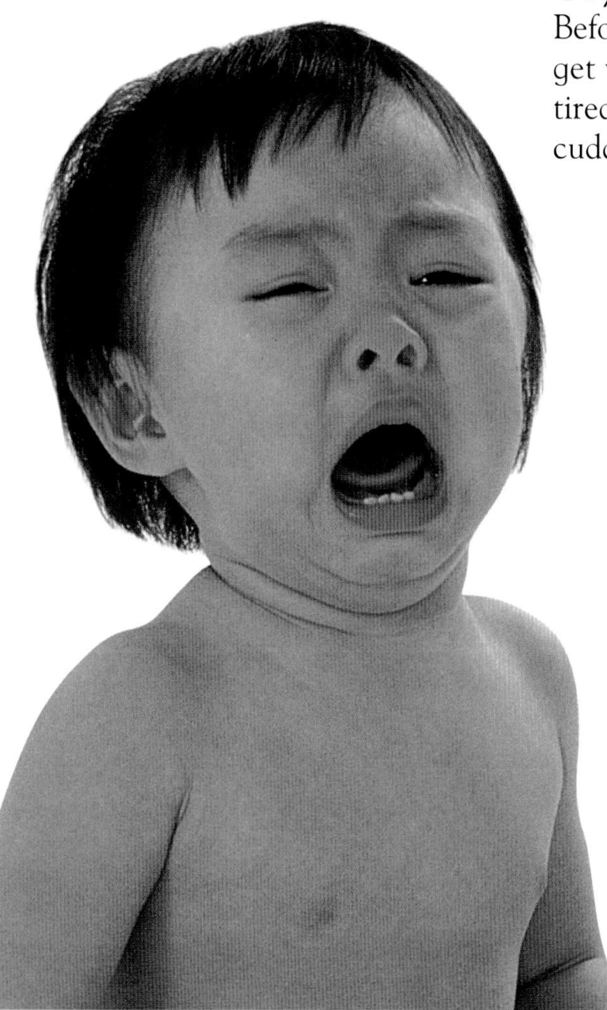

Cry baby
Before she develops language, the only way for a baby to get what she wants is to cry. Babies cry when they are tired, hungry, uncomfortable, or when they just need a cuddle or something to play with.

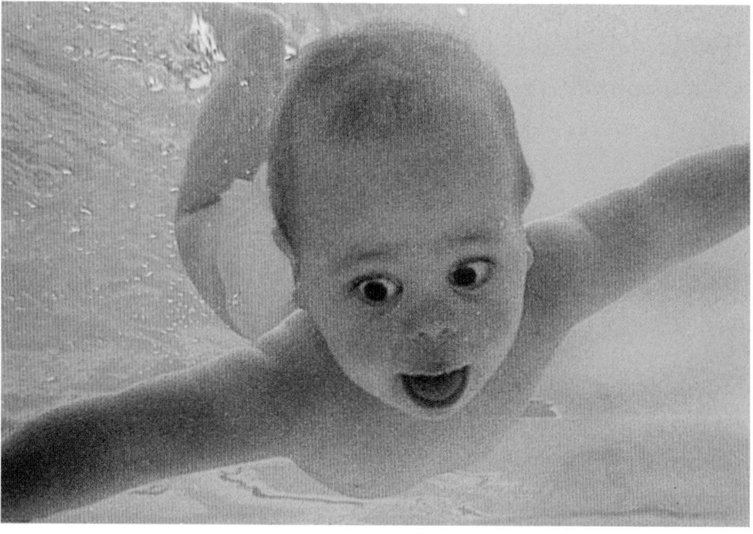

Reflex actions
Reflexes are muscle contractions that happen without us trying. Young babies submerged in water automatically close a muscle to stop water from entering their lungs. This reflex disappears after the age of three months.

Seemore Says

Hungry brain! 60% of the food energy a baby takes in goes to feed its brain. The brain has to find room in its memory for the millions of sights, sounds, and smells that bombard it every day. At the same time, it must gain control over the body. In your first year, your brain increases its volume by two and a half times.

Babies need sleep

Newborn babies have to sleep about 16 hours out of every 24. Half of that time is spent with the intense brain activity that accompanies dreams. They wake up every four to six hours to feed until their digestive systems can store enough food to fuel their bodies through the night.

Cute babies

Babies from many species share the same features of cuteness that make adults want to protect them. Baby humans and animals share curiosity and eagerness to learn. They find out about the things around them by playing with them and putting them in their mouths.

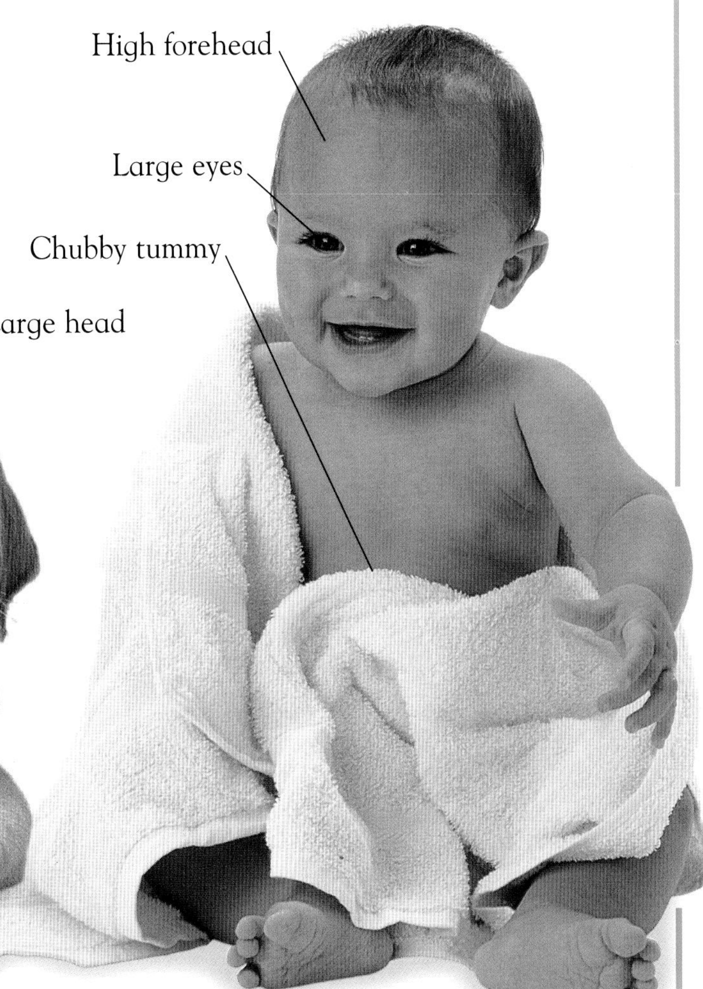

How you learn

In your first ten years, your brain commits to memory millions of sights, sounds, and smells while slowly learning to control your muscles. It enables you to learn a language, acquire a personality, and learn how to get along with others. It's no wonder a human's brain takes longer to mature than that of any other animal on earth.

NEWBORN BRAINS HAVE RELATIVELY FEW CONNECTIONS.

GROWING BRAINS DEVELOP COMPLEX NETWORKS.

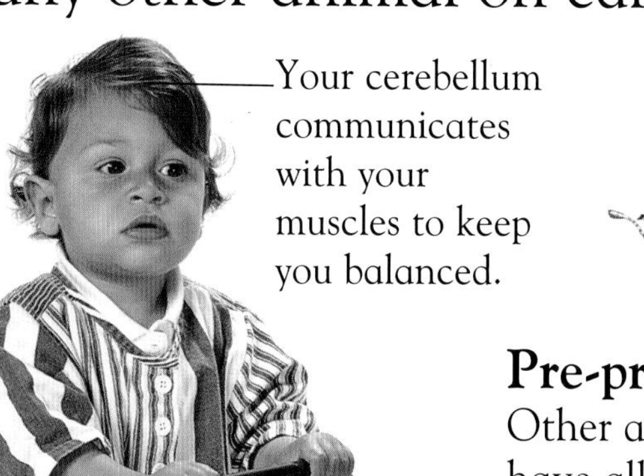

Your cerebellum communicates with your muscles to keep you balanced.

Pre-programmed knowledge

Other animals, such as this ladybug, have all the information they need from day one! Knowledge you're born with is called instinct.

Pathways of thoughts

Scientists believe that the brain increases its learning capacity by forging new pathways for its electrical impulses. When you were born, each brain cell was hooked up to about 2,500 neurons. That number increases to 15,000 by the time you're eleven years old.

Try it Yourself

Try to say "Papa" without moving your lips or "noon" without moving your tongue. In order for you to be able to speak, your brain has to learn precise and coordinated control over dozens of different muscles.

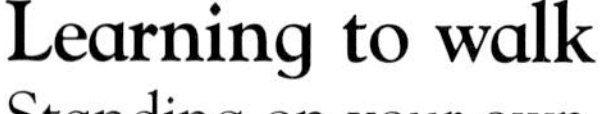

Learning to walk

Standing on your own two feet is one of the trickiest things your body has to learn to do. The brain must stay in constant communication with your muscles to stop you from toppling over.

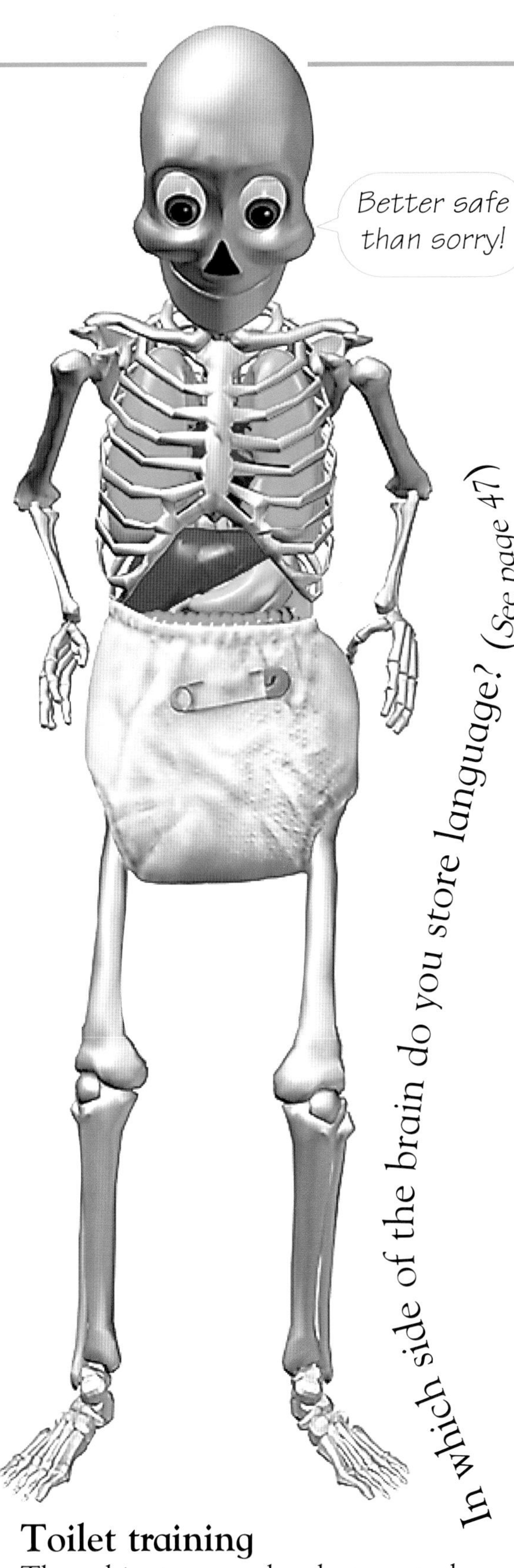
Better safe than sorry!

In which side of the brain do you store language? (See page 47)

Seemore Says

It's much easier to learn a language before the age of six. After that, any new language you acquire is stored in a completely different part of the brain. Children who grow up speaking two languages are "bilingual."

Age 3 years

Age 7 years

Motor control

Gradually, your brain strengthens the connections in its motor control centers to help you achieve precise control over muscles used for tasks such as drawing. It takes up to eight years for motor control skills to develop completely.

Child prodigy

Some people seem to be born with special talents, although hard work is always needed to develop their skills. The composer Wolfgang Mozart published his first music at the age of eight.

MOZART

Growing and changing
How your voice works Vocal cords

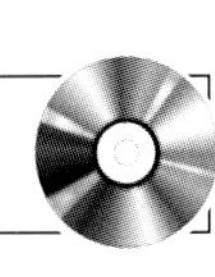

Toilet training

The sphincter muscles that control the bowel and bladder are the last muscles you learn to control. It's amazing that you master speech while still wearing diapers!

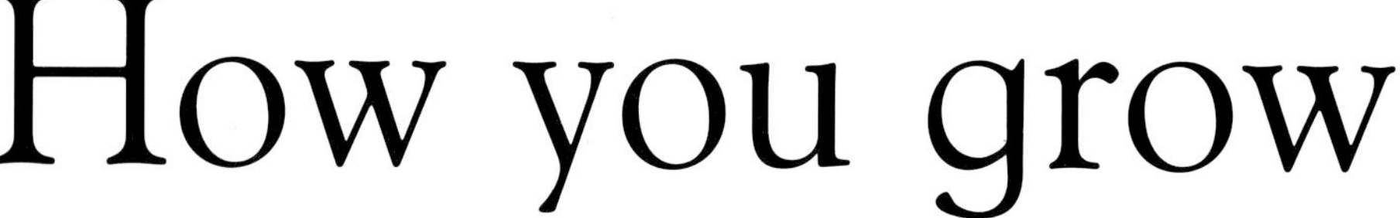

How you grow

Between the ages of two and eighteen, your skeleton roughly doubles its height. The body's other systems stick to the same slow and steady pace. Meanwhile, your body uses messenger proteins, called hormones, to tell your organs when it is time to grow.

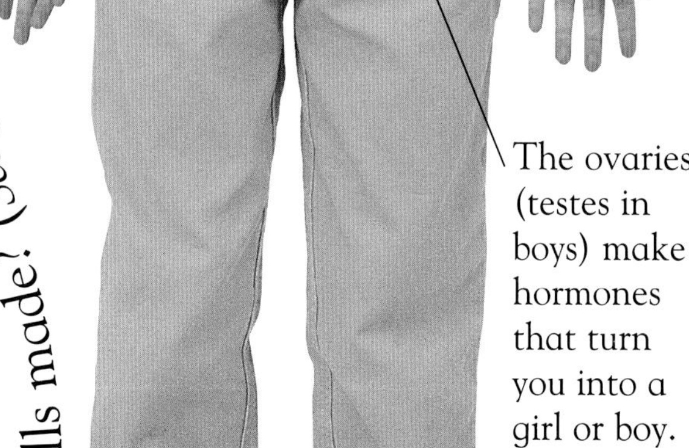

The pituitary gland tells other glands what to do.
The thyroid gland controls the body's use of energy as well as rate of growth.
Adrenal glands give you speed and power when you need it.
The ovaries (testes in boys) make hormones that turn you into a girl or boy.

Endocrine system

Hormones are created in glands found tucked away all over the body. Together they make the endocrine system. These glands are responsible for directing all of the changes that happen in your body over time. The most important hormones which affect growth are produced in the pituitary and thyroid glands.

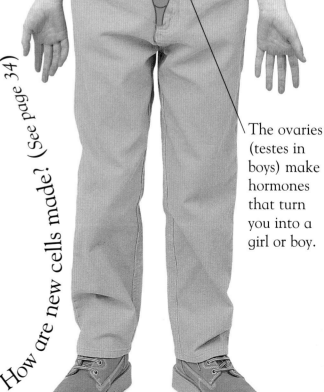

Ask Seemore

What are growing pains?

Many children between the ages of six and twelve feel pain in their calves during the night. Some scientists think these pains are related to sudden spurts of growth.

How are new cells made? (See page 34)

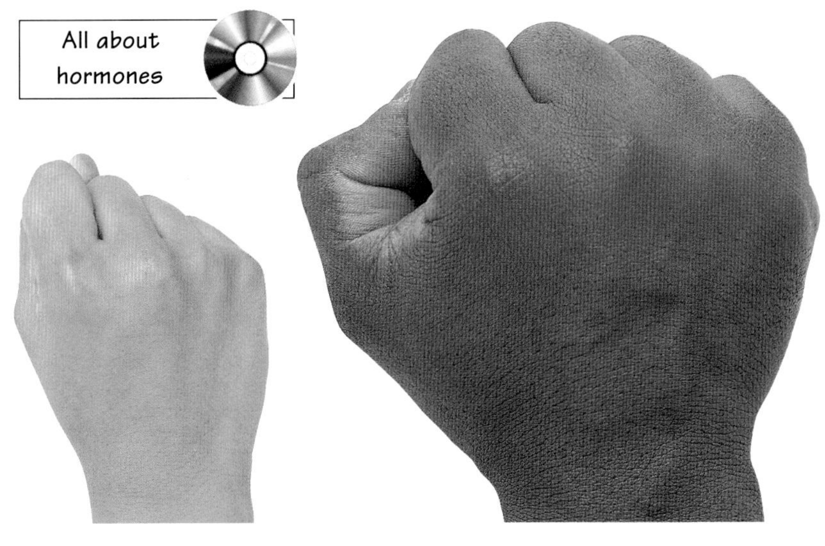
All about hormones

10-YEAR-OLD CHILD

40-YEAR-OLD MAN

Organs keep up

Your heart is about the size of your fist, whatever your age. Your internal organs have to keep growing into adulthood to handle the needs of your larger body.

2
5
8
10

Height proportion

As you grow, your body proportions change. Babies' heads account for a quarter of their height. By the time you're fully grown, your head is only about an eighth of your height. As you get older, your limbs become proportionately longer and you take on a thinner, trimmer shape.

Bone growth

The baby's hand has less bone than the adult's hand because large parts of her skeleton are still growing. The baby's hand is composed of pliable cartilage that doesn't show up on an x-ray (*see page 45*). When bones grow, new cartilage cells pour from a thin layer near the end of each bone called the growth plate. In time, the cartilage is strengthened with calcium and becomes true bone.

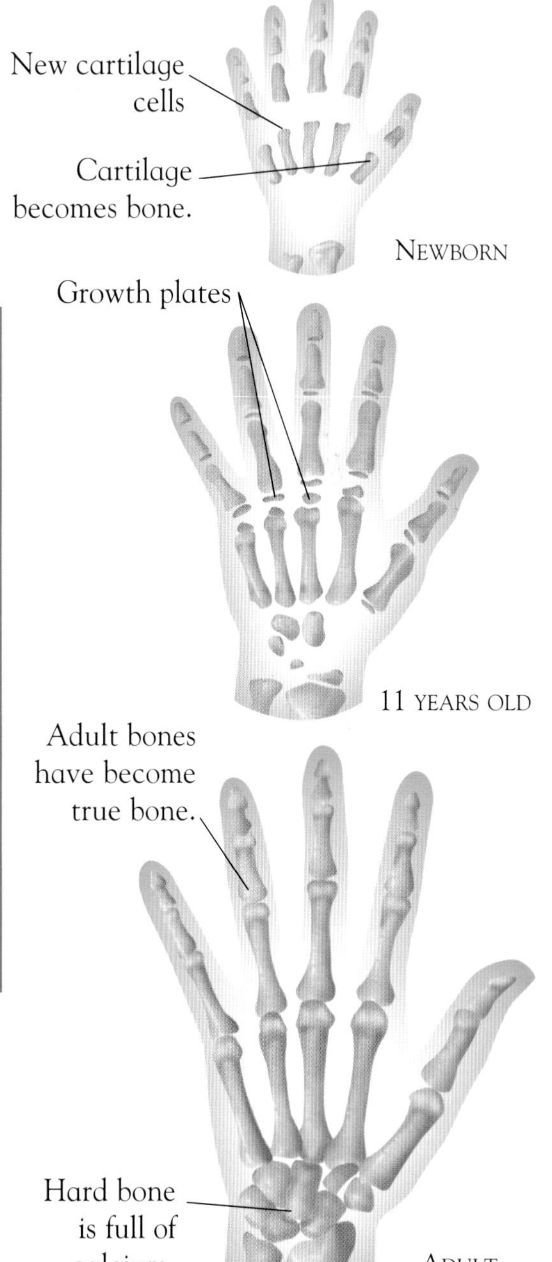
New cartilage cells
Cartilage becomes bone.
Growth plates
Adult bones have become true bone.
Hard bone is full of calcium.

NEWBORN

11 YEARS OLD

ADULT

Becoming a teenager

Human beings reach puberty between the ages of about 11 and 16. During this time, our bodies prepare us for the business of attracting a mate and making babies. However, although we may be physically able to have babies at 14 or 15, most of us will not be mentally prepared for the responsibility of parenthood for many years to come.

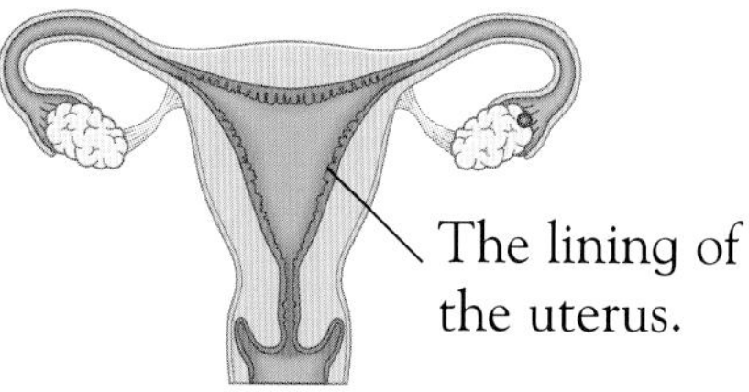

The lining of the uterus.

INSIDE THE UTERUS

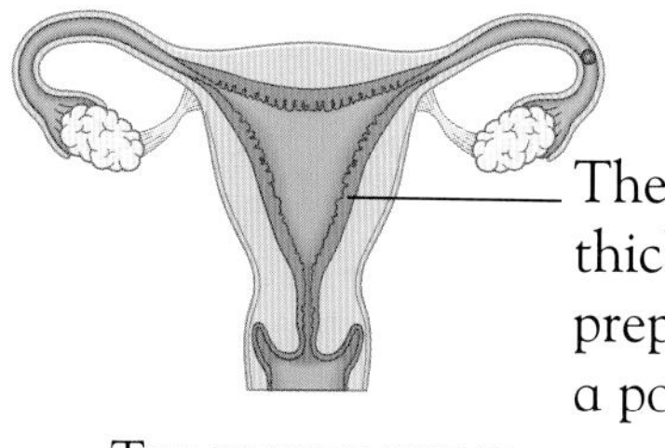

The lining thickens to prepare for a possible pregnancy.

THE UTERUS LINING

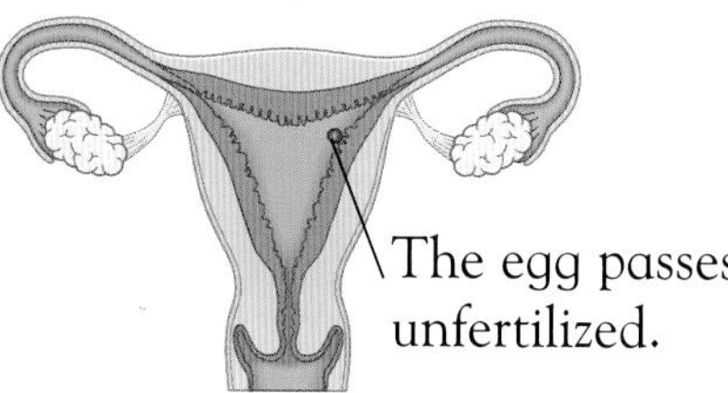

The egg passes unfertilized.

OVULATION

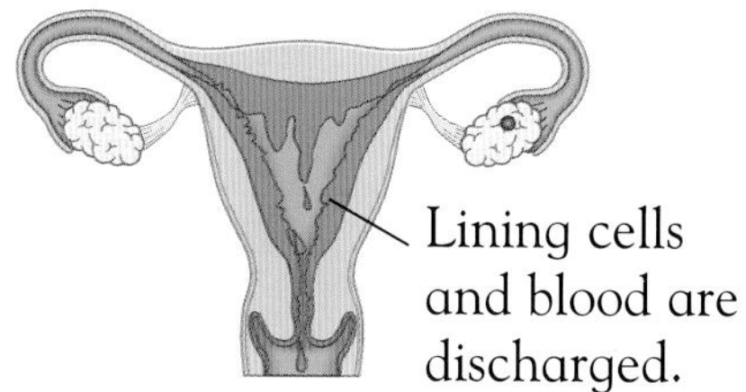

Lining cells and blood are discharged.

THE PERIOD BEGINS

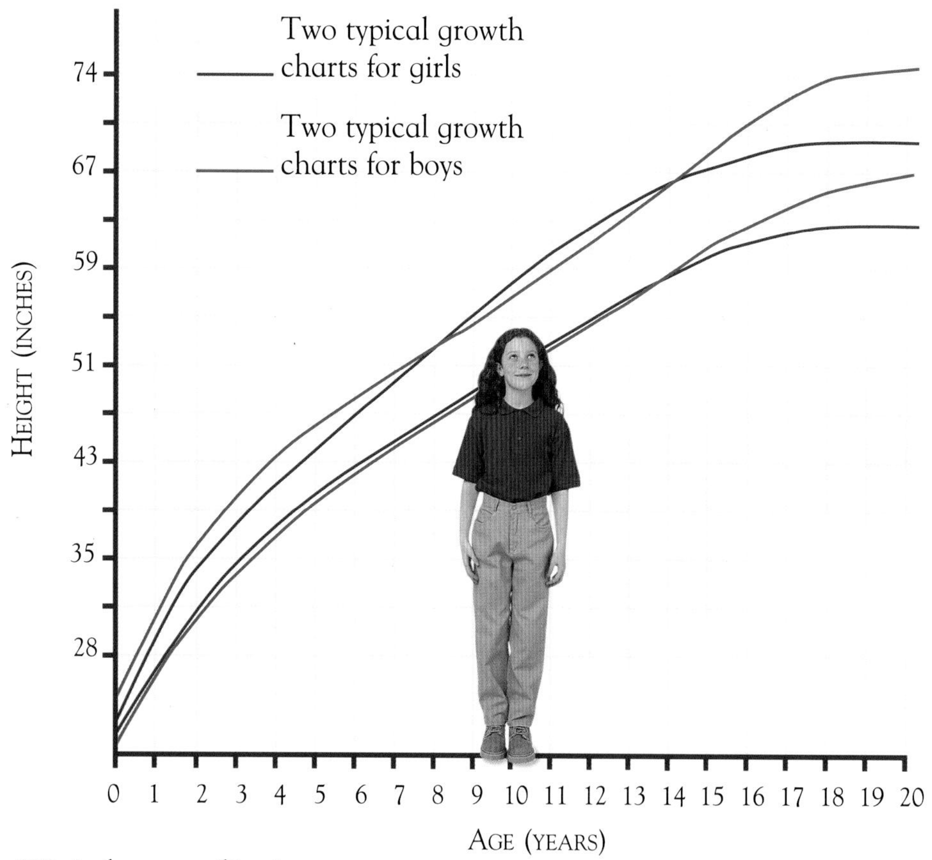

Height prediction

You can predict how tall you will be. Plot your present height on the chart above your age. The gap between you and the example growth lines marked is likely to stay the same for the rest of your growing years.

Menstrual cycle

At puberty, a girl's uterus prepares for a newly fertilized egg each month. Unless pregnancy occurs, the egg passes through the uterus and the extra tissue is discharged with a little blood. Bleeding lasts from three to seven days and is called a menstrual period.

Growing and changing How boys change
How girls change Where babies come from

Seemore Says

When you reach puberty, your skin starts to produce more oil, called sebum. Sebum can block pores and cause pimples. The pus inside a spot is made from the dead white blood cells that fight the infection caused by the pimple.

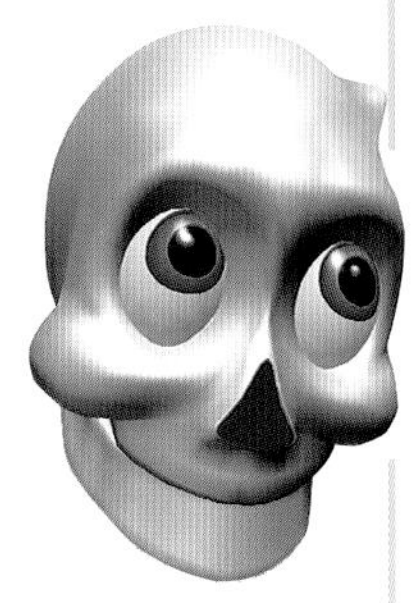

How many sperm cells does one male make in a day? (See page 27)

Becoming an adult

Around the age of 12, the hypothalamus (part of the brain that controls hormones) senses that it's time to make a few changes. It commands ovaries to make estrogen and testes to make testosterone.

First feelings of sexual attraction.

Hair appears under arms.

Cells form milk ducts for future breastfeeding.

Pockets of fat build up around hips and on breasts.

Pelvis changes shape, resulting in broader hips for easier childbirth.

Pubic hair appears around genitals.

Breasts develop and nipples darken.

Ovaries produce the hormone estrogen.

Monthly release of eggs begins.

Pimples may appear.

Facial hair starts to grow.

Pubic hair appears around genitals.

First feelings of sexual attraction.

Vocal cords lengthen, resulting in a deeper voice.

Heart and lungs increase their capacity to get oxygen to the muscles.

Sweat in hairy regions such as armpits gains a fatty ingredient that gives off a smell.

Growth of scrotum allows testes to drop away from the body.

Testes produce the hormone testosterone.

Muscles grow larger and stronger.

Becoming a grown-up

Adolescence is the period in your life that starts with puberty and lasts well into your early 20s. It can be an emotional roller coaster. It's a time for experimentation and fun, but also for important decision making. During this period, you will learn to gain control over your emotions, form lasting friendships, and make choices that will affect the rest of your life.

Who am I?

Adolescence is a time for trying different types of behavior and different ways of dressing. This is part of deciding what sort of person you are, and it can be a lot of fun.

Forming relationships

Adolescence brings with it the first strong feelings of affection and sexual attraction. The kids around you might start dating. Or they might just start acting really strangely around people they've known for years. It takes time to find someone you're compatible with, so relationships between adolescents may last only a few weeks.

Growing and changing

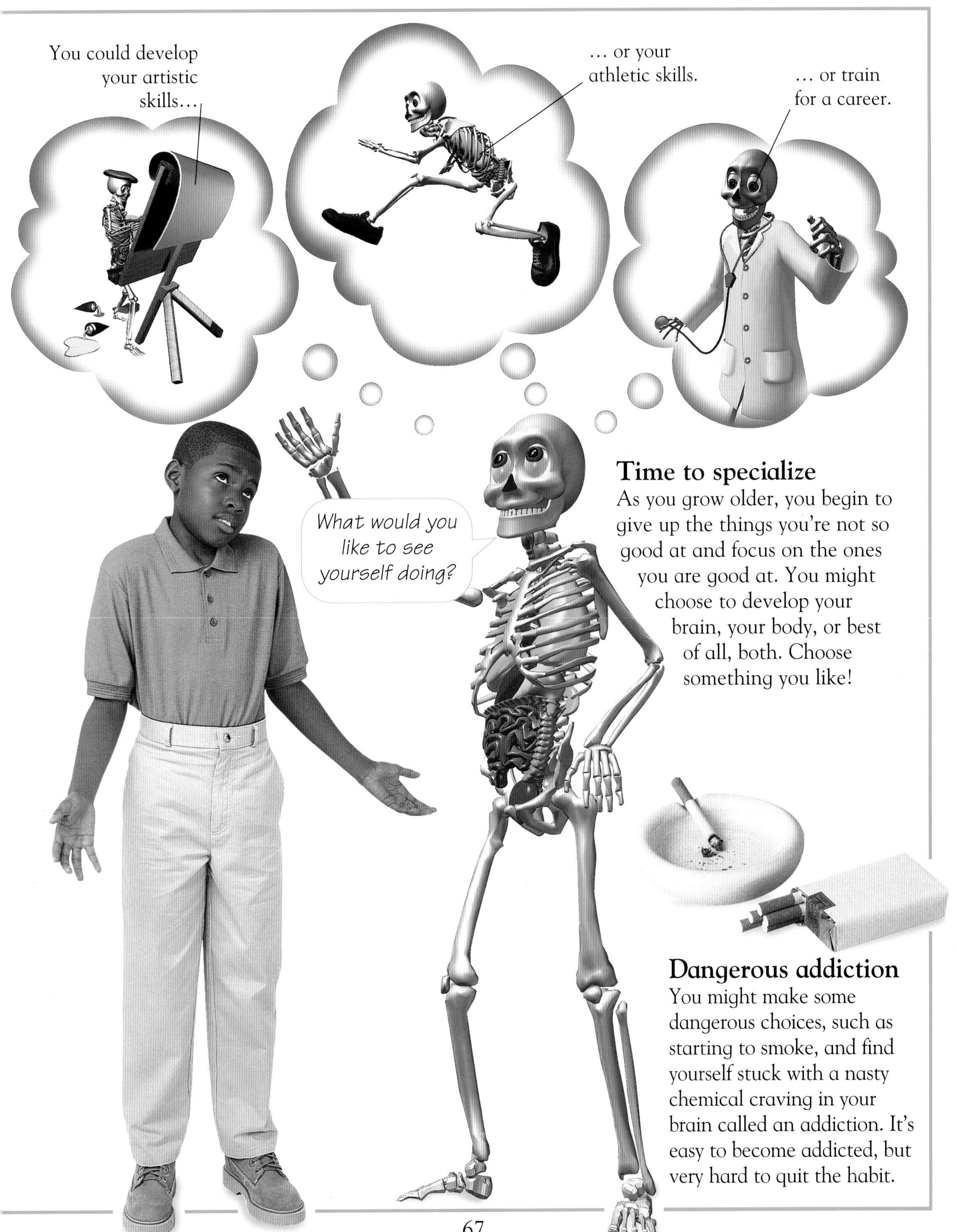
You could develop your artistic skills...
... or your athletic skills.
... or train for a career.
What would you like to see yourself doing?

Time to specialize

As you grow older, you begin to give up the things you're not so good at and focus on the ones you are good at. You might choose to develop your brain, your body, or best of all, both. Choose something you like!

Dangerous addiction

You might make some dangerous choices, such as starting to smoke, and find yourself stuck with a nasty chemical craving in your brain called an addiction. It's easy to become addicted, but very hard to quit the habit.

Growing older

Growing and changing
Growing older

Except for tooth enamel, there are very few cells in your body that are more than ten years old. Luckily, old cells make new cells before they die. But sometimes, mistakes appear in the cells' DNA while they are being copied. Some scientists believe that, after several years, these DNA mistakes build up and our bodies start to show their age.

Aging gracefully

Just because the body is slowing down doesn't mean that it can't do wonderful things. At the age of 77, astronaut John Glenn became the oldest person to travel in space.

Men become apple-shaped.

Women become pear-shaped.

Fat deposits

As people get older they tend to slow down. The fat that once would have been burned off is now stored. Women store fat low down on their hips, while men store it higher up on their tummies.

Menopause

Between the ages of about 50 and 60, a woman goes through menopause. Her ovaries stop producing eggs so she can no longer have babies.

Seemore Says

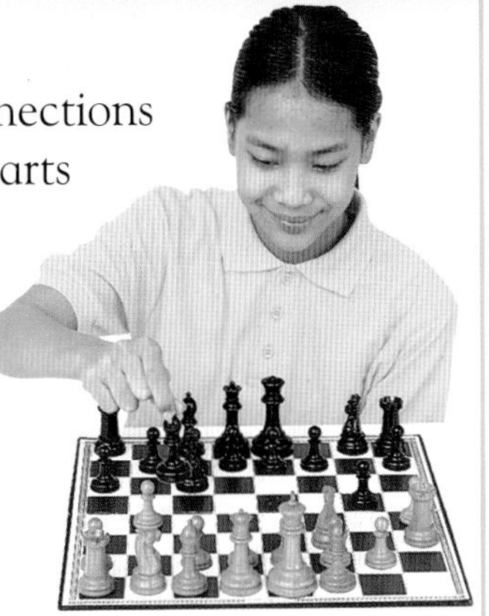

Thousands of nerve cell connections die every day. The process starts when you are just 11 years old and continues all your life. You can help to slow the process down – the more you use your brain, the longer it keeps its connections.

The hormone testosterone stops hair from growing in some men and leads to baldness.

Hair follicles stop making pigment and hair turns white.

Eyes can't focus on things which are near.

Nose and ears continue to grow.

The aging process

With time, the skin gradually loses elastin and collagen, its stretchy proteins. Instead of bouncing back like rubber, the skin starts to wrinkle like paper and droop loosely downward.

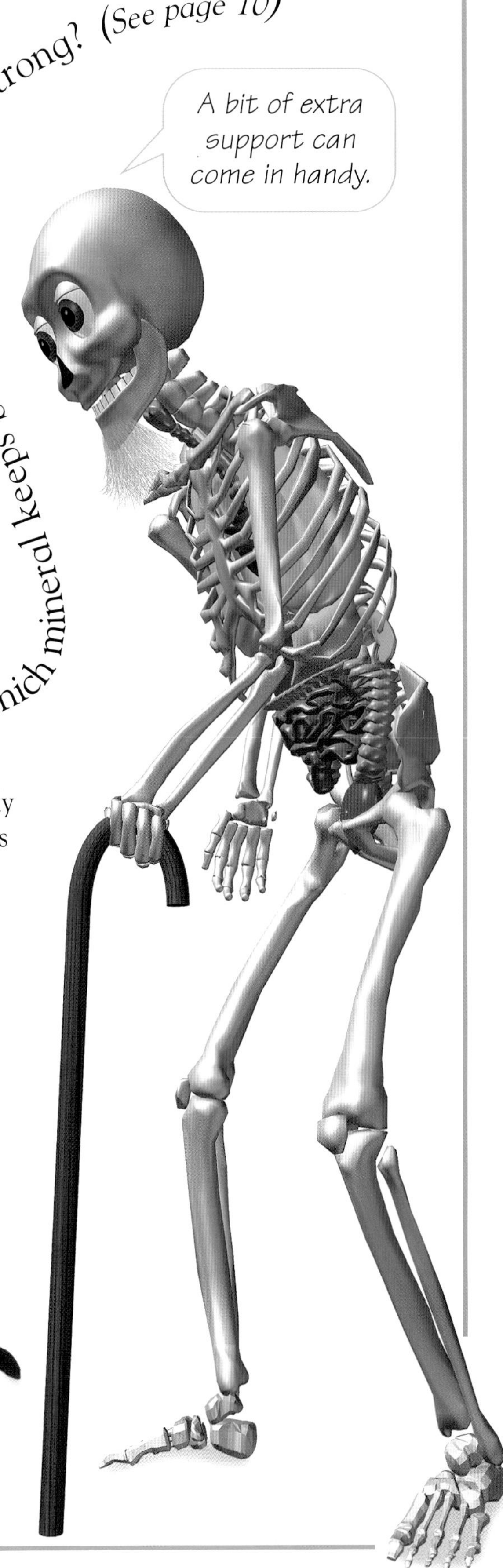

A bit of extra support can come in handy.

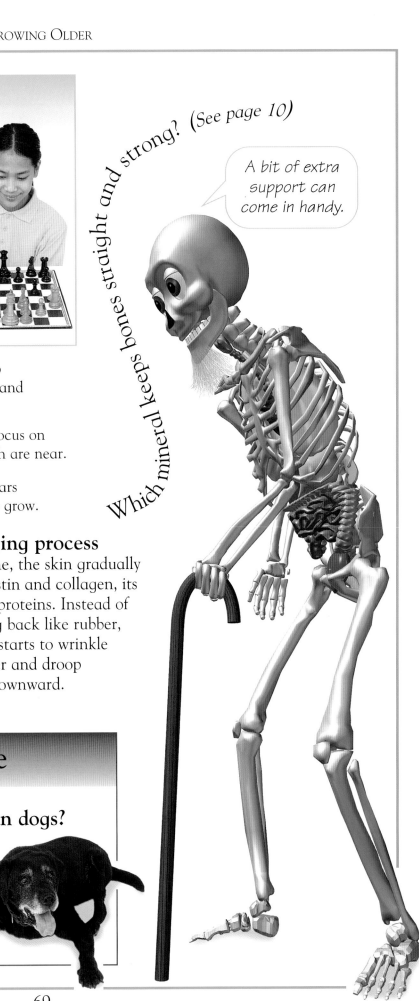

Which mineral keeps bones straight and strong? (See page 10)

Ask Seemore

Why do humans live longer than dogs?

There are many reasons, but scientists think that antioxidants may be responsible. These chemicals protect us from some of the damaging effects oxygen molecules have on our chromosomes.

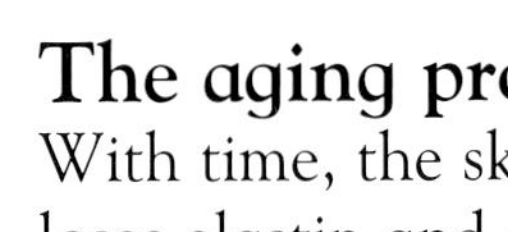

In your lifetime

We all know we have to go sometime. Death is a fact of life. The good news is that life expectancies are getting longer and longer as people learn more about health and scientists find cures for killer diseases. In the first 75 years alone, the average person will have ...

...spent one year traveling by car.
The exact amount of time you spend in a car depends on your circumstance, but it will probably increase as time goes on. Try to walk or bicycle whenever you can and keep that body moving!

...spent three years watching TV.
How many hours of TV do you watch each week? You can learn a lot from TV programs, but fresh air and exercise do more for your body.

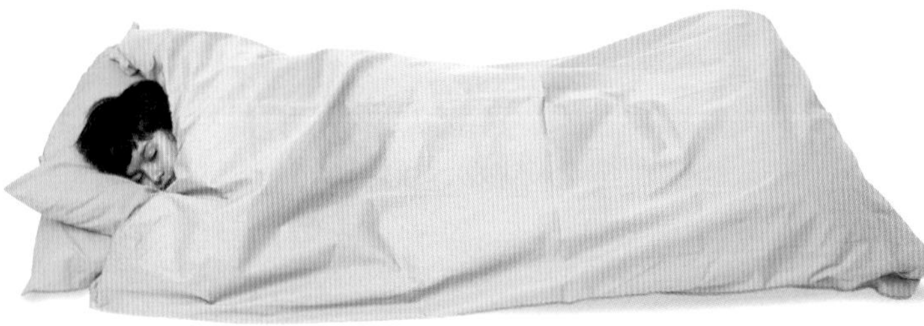

...spent 22 years sleeping.
22 years asleep might seem like a huge waste of time, after all, it's nearly a third of your entire life! However, this time is essential for your body's repair mechanisms.

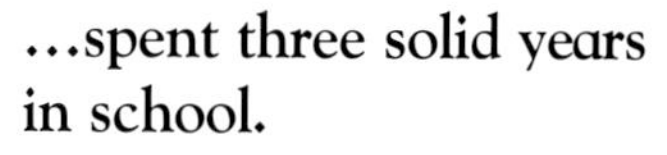

...spent three solid years in school.
Seven hours a day, five days a week – school takes up most of your time when you're young. Learn as much as you can while your brain is still growing.

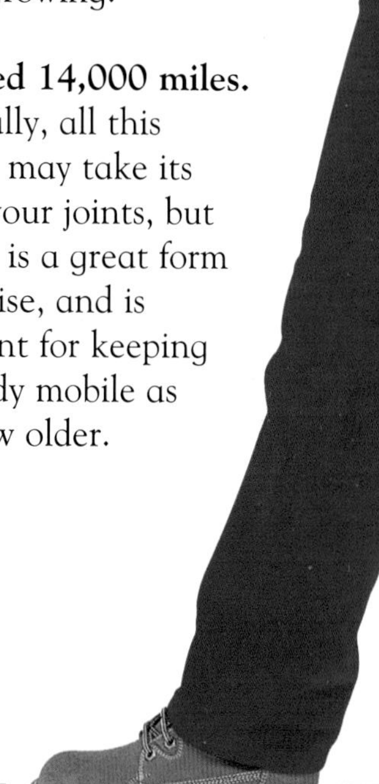

...walked 14,000 miles.
Eventually, all this walking may take its toll on your joints, but walking is a great form of exercise, and is important for keeping your body mobile as you grow older.

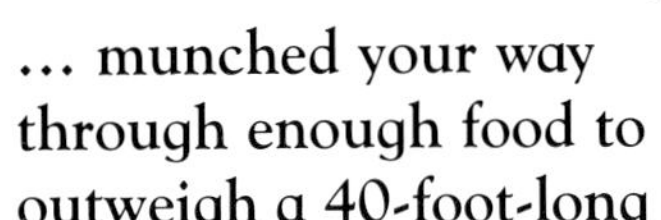

... munched your way through enough food to outweigh a 40-foot-long (13-meter-long) whale. Keep a food diary for a week. You can then figure out what kinds of food you eat, as well as how much.

... lost enough sweat to fill a large tanker truck. If you're getting rid of that much water, you need to make sure you keep your tank filled up. Drinking water is good for you.

... breathed in and out enough air to fill the world's largest gas tank. Focus on your breathing from time to time. Long, deep breaths are better than short, shallow breaths.

... made enough excrement to a fill large cement mixer. Well, if you eat all that food, you're bound to produce a lot of waste!

... made enough urine to fill 500 bathtubs. More water! Monitor your trips to the bathroom for a day and you'll soon see how a lifetime's urine reaches that level. The more you drink, the more you'll need to go, but this is the body's way of cleansing your system.

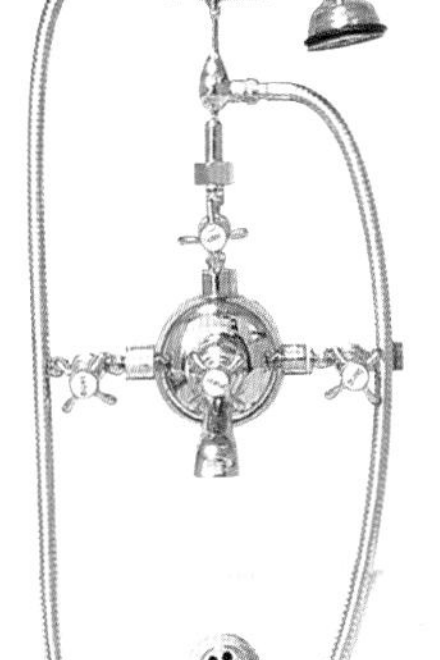

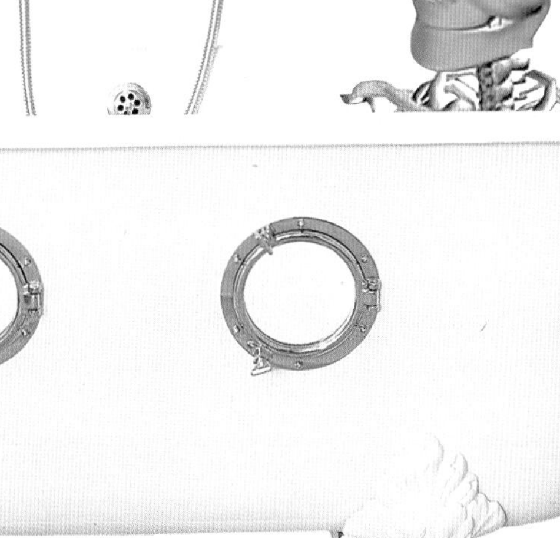

... And that's not all. You will also have...

... made 500 trillion red blood cells.

... grown 600 miles (1,000 km) of hair.

... changed all your cells repeatedly (except the enamel on your teeth and most of your brain cells).

... cried 12 buckets worth of tears.

... produced enough snot to fill seven bathtubs.

Body maintenance

What kind of body would you like to have? There are some things about your body you just can't change, and some that you can. All bodies have their limitations – for example, you can't do much about your height. Still, no matter what its limits are, your body is the most valuable possession you will ever have. How well you treat it is up to you.

The choices you make regarding the food you eat, whether or not you exercise, and the risks you take in life all have an impact on the health of your body and how well it lasts.

Of course, they're all my own teeth!

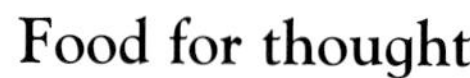

Food for thought
A balanced diet is one of the best ways to keep your body healthy. By all means, go for that burger, but remember to eat your greens as well.

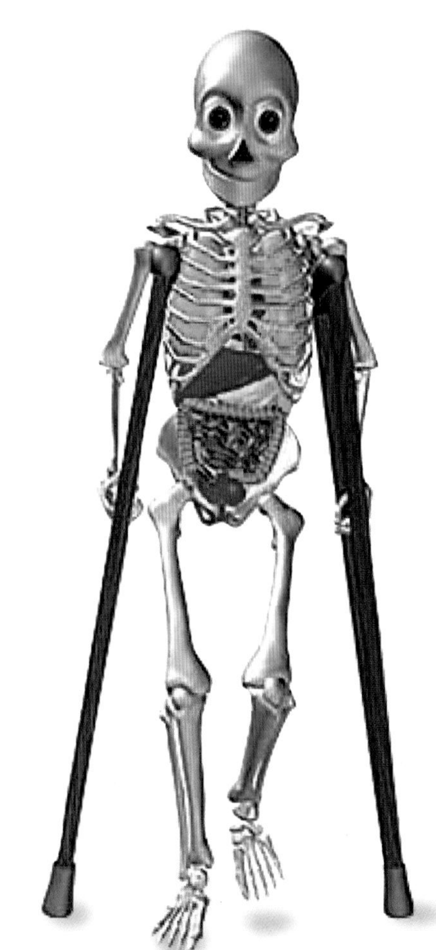

Leave it to the professionals
There may be a time in your life when you need help from the medical profession. Or you might be the one to offer first aid.

Fit for life
Regular exercise is the best habit you can choose. Being fit is good for your mental health as well as your physical wellbeing.

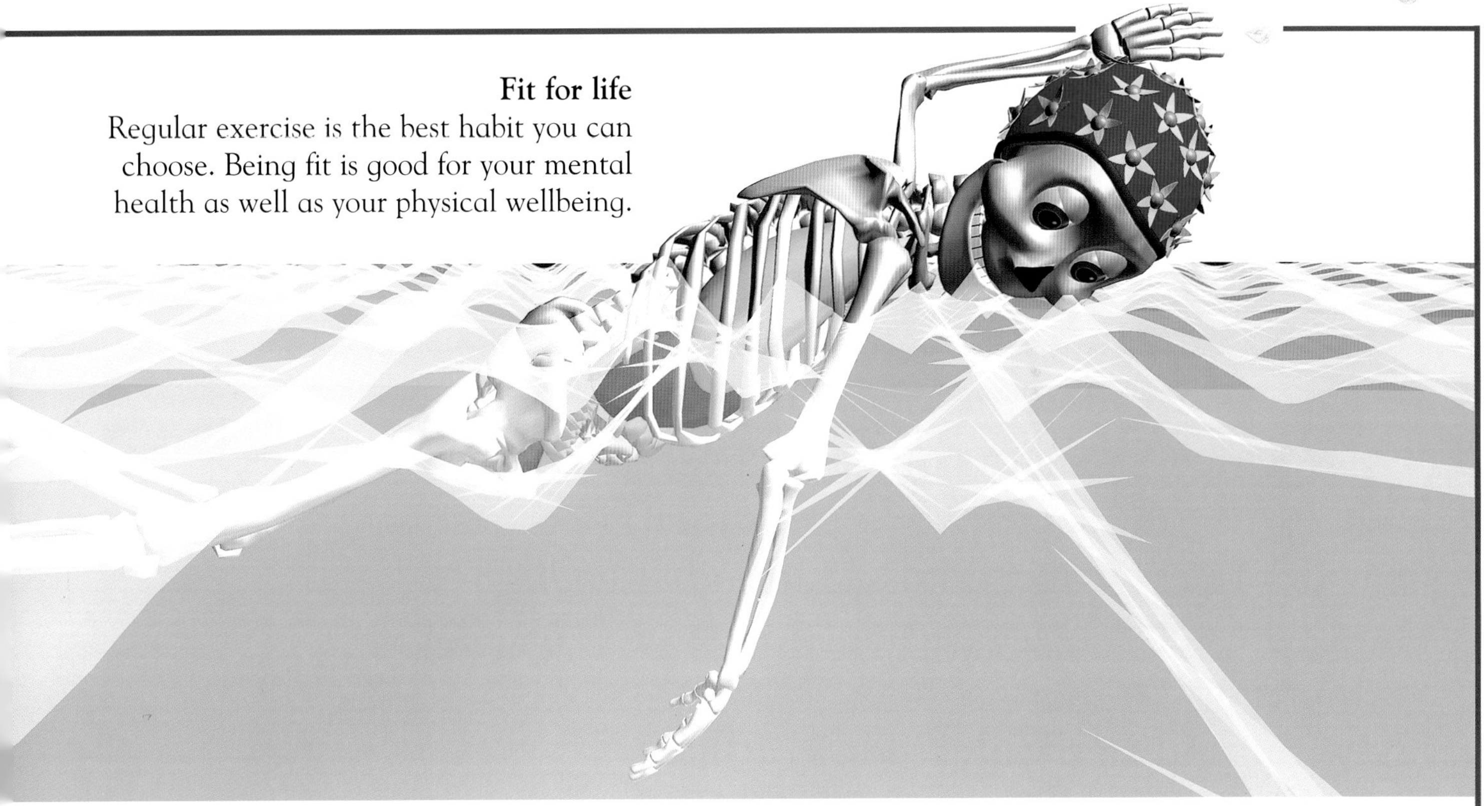

Making choices
Whatever you choose to be in your life, healthy attitudes can be easily incorporated into your lifestyle.

You could be an opera singer …

… or a soccer player.

… or a fitness instructor.

Choose health

Here are five reasons to choose health now:

- You won't be ill as often
- You'll do better at sports
- You'll look better
- Your brain will work better
- You'll develop good habits which will set you up for a long and happy life.

A balanced diet

Why do we eat? There are several reasons. Food contains fats and carbohydrates (sugars and starches) that your body turns into energy to keep going. Food also provides the raw materials your body needs to build new cells. You need nutrients, such as vitamins and minerals, to keep your body running smoothly and healthily. Another reason to eat is so obvious it almost goes without saying – good food tastes great!

CANDY, CHOCOLATE, ICE CREAM, AND CHIPS

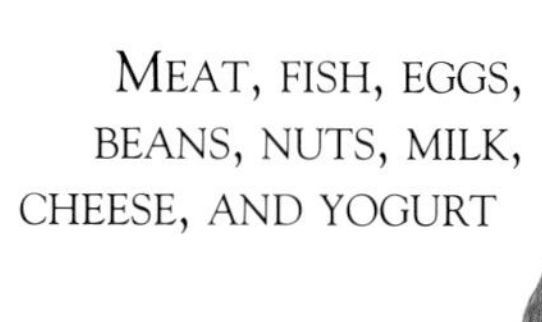

MEAT, FISH, EGGS,
BEANS, NUTS, MILK,
CHEESE, AND YOGURT

Oh, why couldn't they put chocolate at the bottom?

FRESH FRUIT AND VEGETABLES

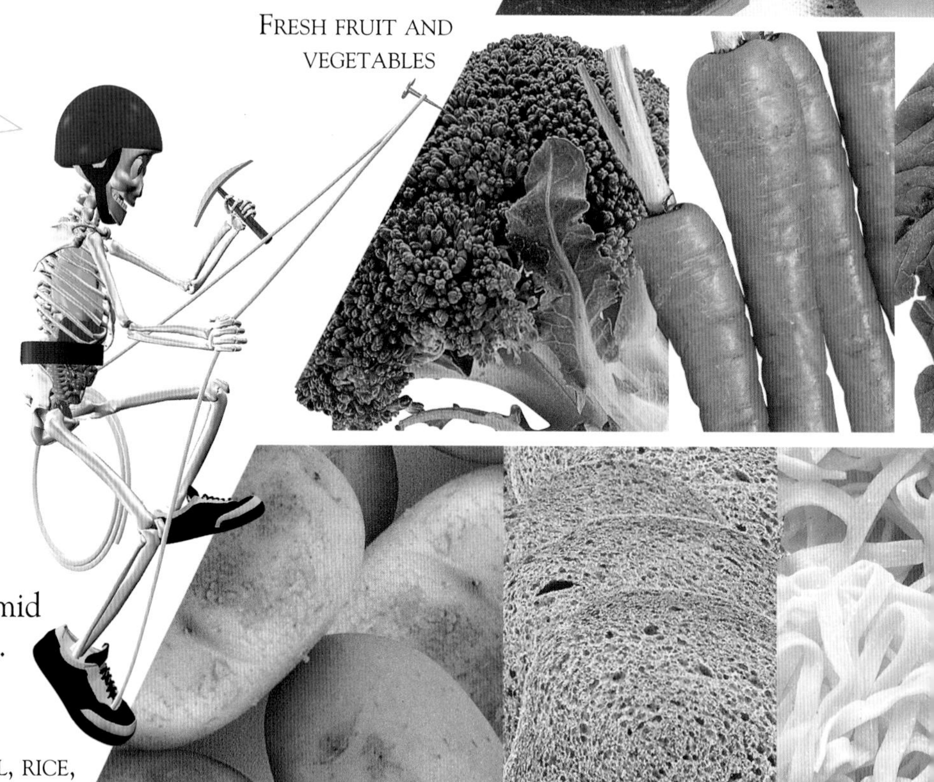

The food pyramid

Your body relies on eating lots of different foods in order to get the nutrients it needs. This food pyramid tells you what proportion of each type of food you should be eating. You should eat only a little of the things at the top of the pyramid but lots of the things at the bottom.

GRAINS, PASTA, CEREAL, RICE, AND SOME FORMS OF POTATO

Seemore Says

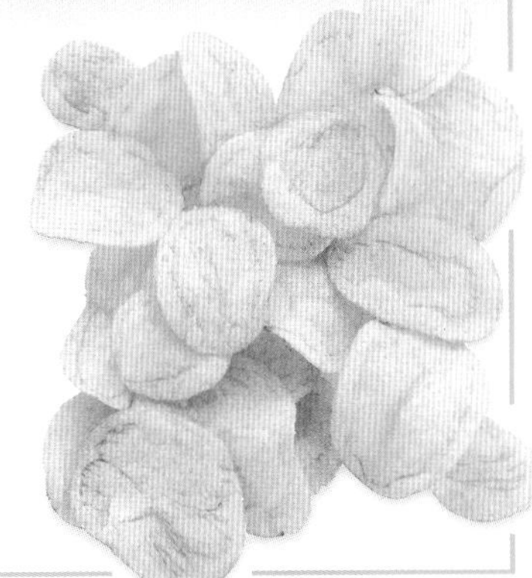

Although potatoes are vegetables, they go to the bottom of the pyramid, because their high starch content makes them a great source of slow-release energy. But they go straight to the top when they're fried in oil to make chips or fries!

Butter, cream, oil, and grease are mostly made of fat.

Sweet and fatty foods give a quick burst of energy, but too many can slow you down.

High-protein foods help your body to grow and replace dead cells.

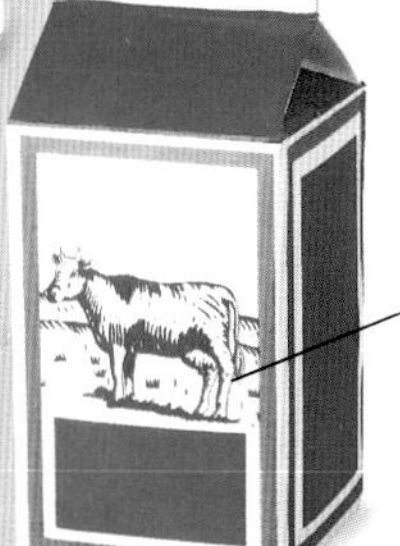

Dairy foods are rich in proteins, vitamins, and calcium for strong bones.

Which minerals are in the body? (See page 6)

Fruits and vegetables are high in vitamins and minerals. They clean your digestive system and help you stay free of disease.

Complex carbohydrates are starches found in grains. They are slow to break down, so they release their energy steadily throughout the day.

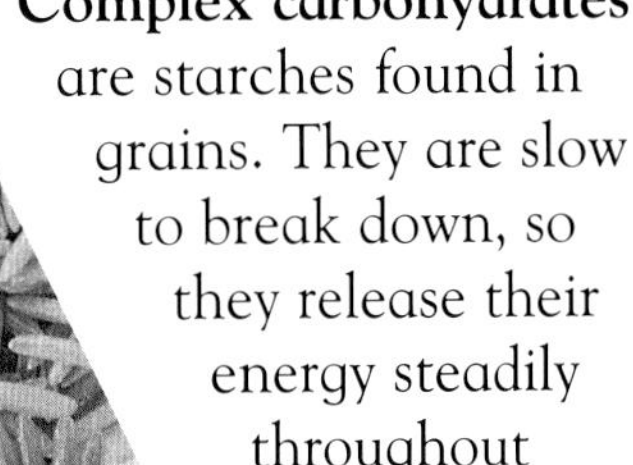

Thirsty work

Unlike a camel, you couldn't survive more than a couple of days without replenishing your water supplies. Juice, milk, and soft drinks are mostly water. But plain water is the only drink with 100% thirst-quenching properties.

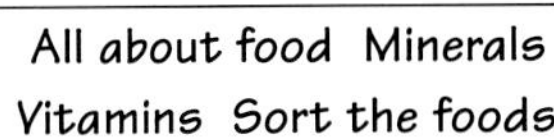

All about food Minerals
Vitamins Sort the foods

Food is energy

All machines need fuel to make them go. Your body is fueled by the food you eat. Foods that are rich in butter, oil, and fats are packed with energy – sometimes more than you need. The more you exercise, the more fuel you need, but if you take in more fuel than you can use every day, your body responds by becoming fatter.

Calorie counting

The amount of energy in food is measured in calories. People burn about 2,000 calories during an average day – but the exact amount depends on your size and how active you are. Big people burn more calories than small people.

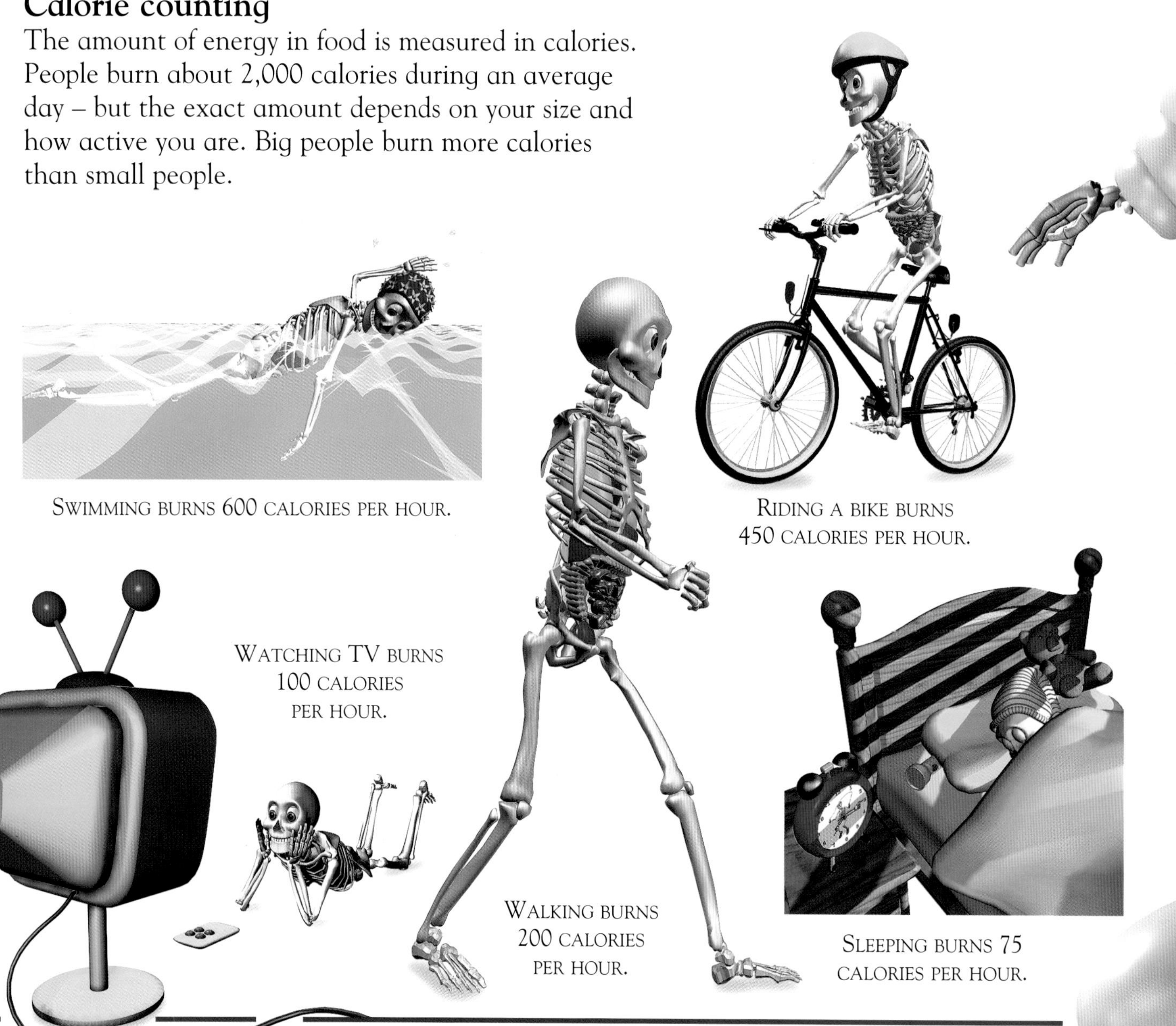

SWIMMING BURNS 600 CALORIES PER HOUR.

RIDING A BIKE BURNS 450 CALORIES PER HOUR.

WATCHING TV BURNS 100 CALORIES PER HOUR.

WALKING BURNS 200 CALORIES PER HOUR.

SLEEPING BURNS 75 CALORIES PER HOUR.

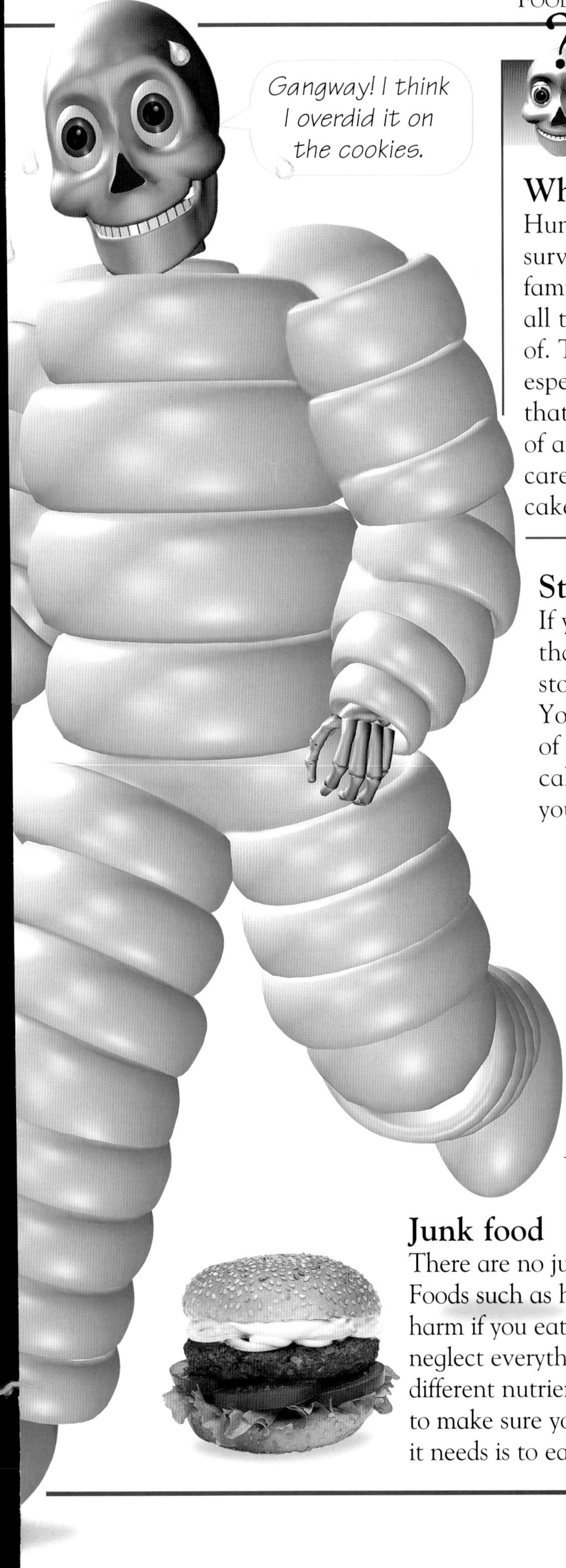

Gangway! I think I overdid it on the cookies.

Ask Seemore

Why are fatty foods so tasty?

Human tastes were molded with survival in mind. To live through famine and war, we need to grab all the calories we can get hold of. That's why fatty foods taste especially good. This means that those of us with plenty of available food need to be careful not to overdo the cakes and chips.

Storing energy

If you take in more calories than you need, your body stores them for another day. You store energy as molecules of fat. If you use more calories than you eat, you will lose fat.

How does the body make energy from food? (See page 38)

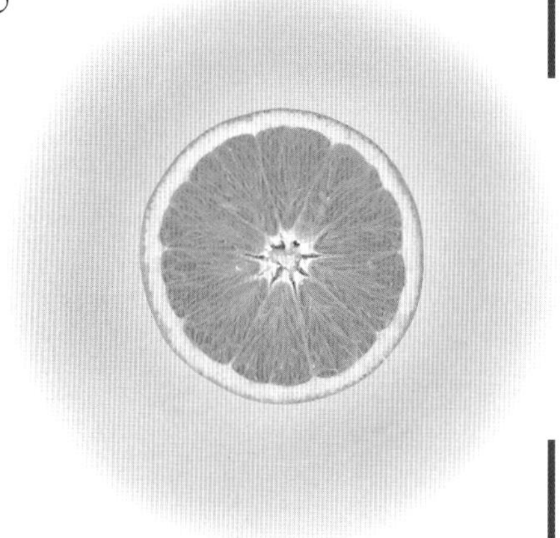

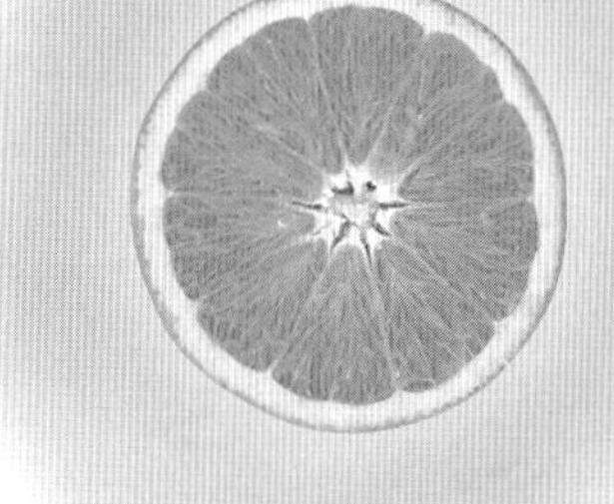

Sun's energy

During photosynthesis, plants harness the Sun's energy to build energy-storing molecules called carbohydrates. When we digest these carbohydrates from fruit and vegetables, the energy is released into our bodies.

Junk food

There are no junk foods, just junk diets. Foods such as hamburgers only do you harm if you eat too many of them and neglect everything else. Every food has different nutrients to offer. The only way to make sure your body gets the nutrients it needs is to eat different kinds of food.

Keeping fit

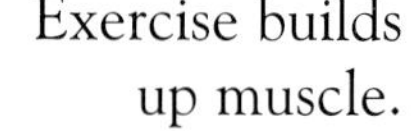

Exercise builds up muscle.

Being physically fit is also called being "in shape." Do you know what "shape" fitness takes? There are three sides to physical fitness: strength, stamina, and flexibility. If you want a really fit body, you must develop all three sides equally by participating in sports or active forms of fun like bike riding or dancing. You only get one body, so why not keep it as healthy as it can be?

Increase your stamina

If you are fit, you have more stamina than an unfit person. This means your lungs can draw in more oxygen, and your heart can pump lots more blood to get that oxygen to your muscles. If you bicycle to school, rather than getting a lift, you'll find your strength and stamina slowly improve.

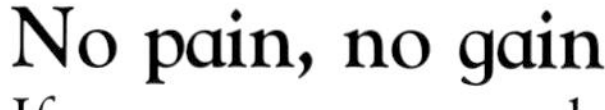

No pain, no gain

If you use your muscles until they're tired, they respond by growing bigger and stronger. Don't push them too hard, though. You might get an injury, and then you won't be able to use the muscles for days. Jogging, running, and swimming are good for building strength and stamina.

A strong heart and lungs get energy and oxygen to the muscles quickly.

Keeping healthy
Taking exercise

Exercise strengthens you while improving your endurance.

Seemore Says

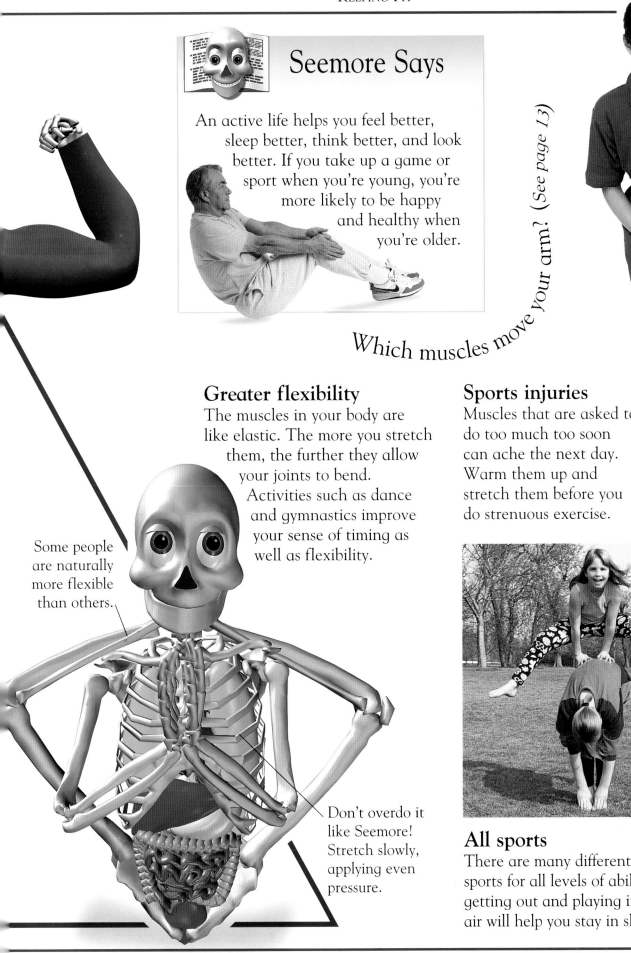

An active life helps you feel better, sleep better, think better, and look better. If you take up a game or sport when you're young, you're more likely to be happy and healthy when you're older.

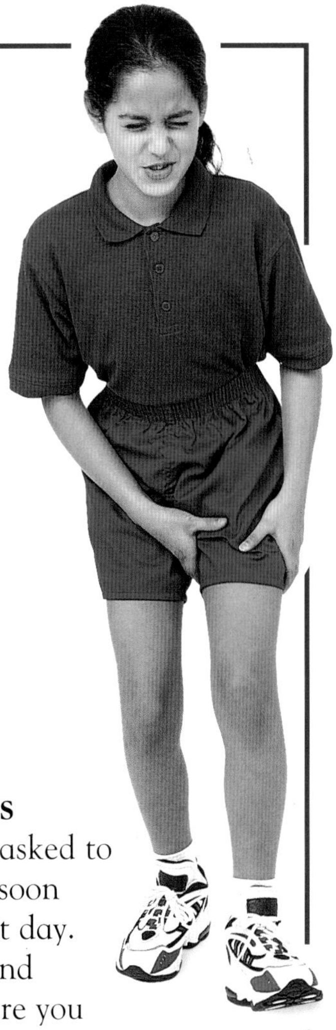

Which muscles move your arm? (See page 13)

Greater flexibility

The muscles in your body are like elastic. The more you stretch them, the further they allow your joints to bend. Activities such as dance and gymnastics improve your sense of timing as well as flexibility.

Some people are naturally more flexible than others.

Don't overdo it like Seemore! Stretch slowly, applying even pressure.

Sports injuries

Muscles that are asked to do too much too soon can ache the next day. Warm them up and stretch them before you do strenuous exercise.

All sports

There are many different kinds of sports for all levels of ability. Just getting out and playing in the fresh air will help you stay in shape.

Around the clock

The hypothalamus, one of the hormone-producing glands inside your brain, has its own internal clock. It automatically understands what your body needs at different times of the day, in order to stay healthy. So, pay attention when your body tells you that it wants exercise, food, or rest. The hypothalamus knows best!

Around and around
The body has a cycle of activity and rest that repeats every 24 hours (or each single rotation of the Earth). The pineal gland in the brain, sometimes called the "third eye," is sensitive to sunlight and keeps your hypothalamus clock in sync with the cycles of day and night.

7:00 am Wake up
The hypothalamus wakes your brain. Movement makes your heart rate and blood pressure rise.

8:00 am Breakfast
Your digestive juices start flowing. The hypothalamus tells you it's time to eat.

9:00 am School
Your brain is now at its most alert and efficient.

5:00 pm Homework
It's time to flex your brain again.

6:00 pm Dinner
You can replenish some of the calories burned off during the day.

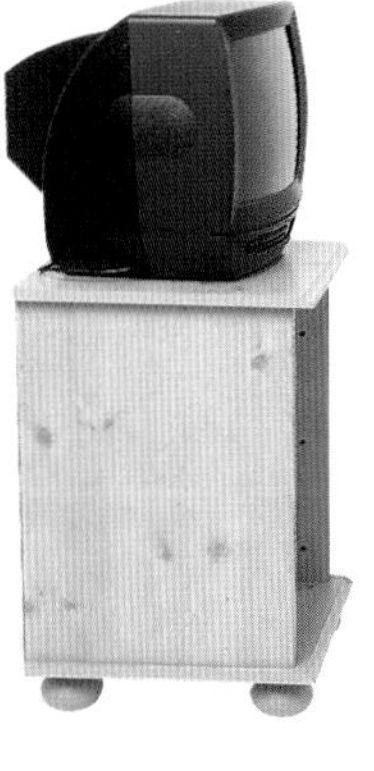

8:00 pm Relax
As it gets dark, the hypothalamus sends out a "slow down" message. It's time to start winding down after your busy day.

Ask Seemore

Why do you need more sleep when you're young?

Childhood is a time of new experiences and rapid learning. Some scientists believe the brain needs the time you are asleep to sort out all the new information.

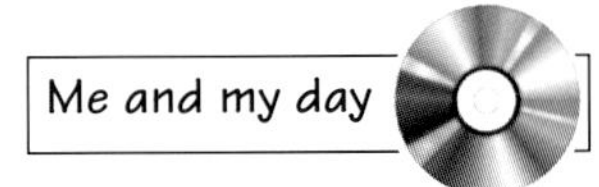

Jet lag

If you travel to a different continent in an airplane your body might get confused about what time it is. One gland is saying "sleep" while the other is saying "wake up!" It may take a few days for your hypothalamus to reset your clock.

11:00 am Snack
Take an energy infusion.

11:15 am Break
The thyroid gland controls your use of energy. Time to burn some calories!

1:00 pm Lunch
The hypothalamus tells you that it's time to fuel up again.

2:00 pm In class
Your brain activity slows as more blood is shunted down to help with the digestion of lunch.

9:00 pm Time for bed
You've washed your face and brushed your teeth, so lights out! You need some sleep.

10.00 pm Sleep
REM (rapid eye movement) sleep occurs about four times a night as your brain enters a highly active dream phase.
12.00 am Brain energy is very low between dream phases.
3.00 am Body temperature falls. Heart slows. Urine production decreases.

Keeping clean

Keeping clean
Sneezing

To germs, your body is a perfect breeding ground. The best strategy for avoiding disease is to simply stay away from germs. That's not always easy because you can't see them coming. You can, however, predict where germs are lurking and do your best to avoid them by sticking to some simple rules of hygiene.

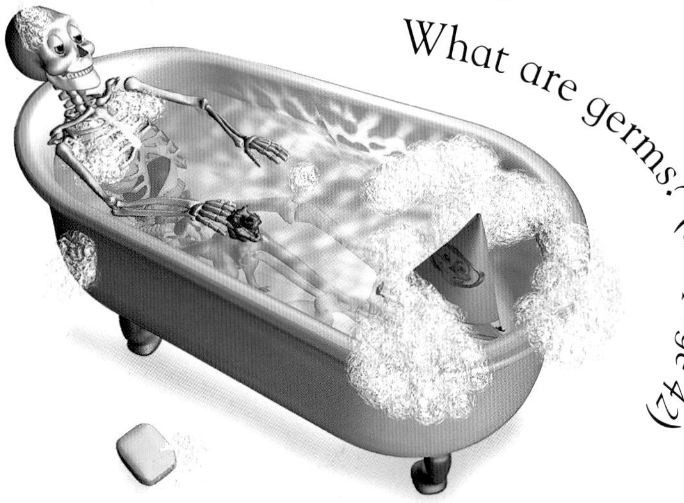

What are germs? (See page 42)

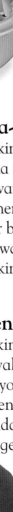

Rub-a-dub dub

Your skin has millions of bacteria all over it. If you don't want "BO" (body odor), keep them in control with regular baths or showers. Soapy water washes away dead skin cells and germs.

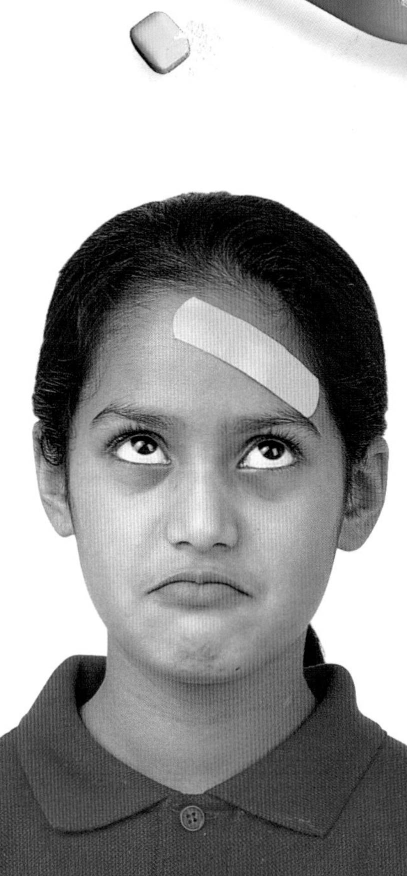

Prevent infection

Your skin provides you with a thick wall against infection. When you cut or scrape the skin, you open the door to germs. Bandages protect wounds from germs while the skin heals.

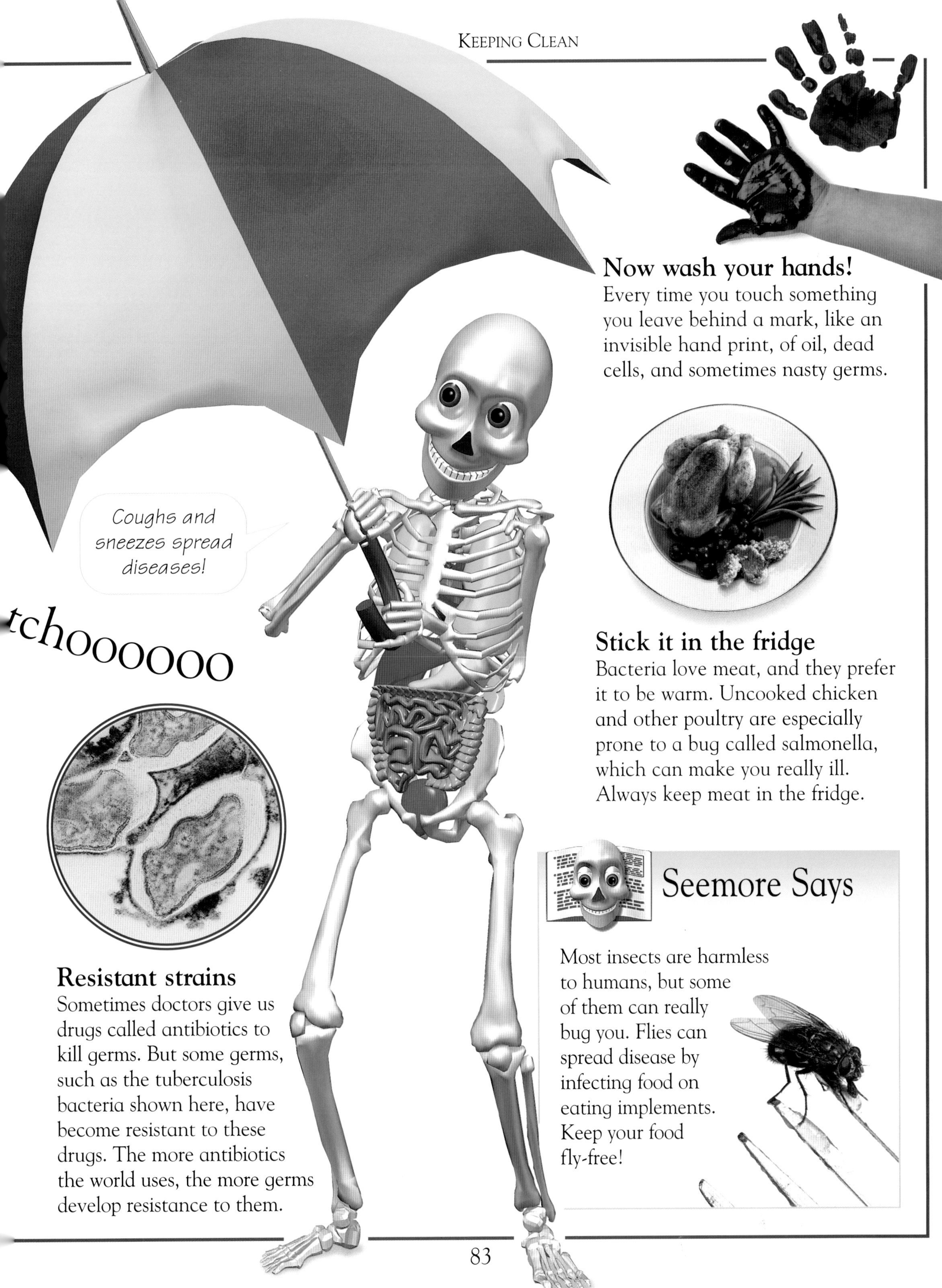
Coughs and sneezes spread diseases!
tchoooooo
Seemore Says

Now wash your hands!

Every time you touch something you leave behind a mark, like an invisible hand print, of oil, dead cells, and sometimes nasty germs.

Stick it in the fridge

Bacteria love meat, and they prefer it to be warm. Uncooked chicken and other poultry are especially prone to a bug called salmonella, which can make you really ill. Always keep meat in the fridge.

Resistant strains

Sometimes doctors give us drugs called antibiotics to kill germs. But some germs, such as the tuberculosis bacteria shown here, have become resistant to these drugs. The more antibiotics the world uses, the more germs develop resistance to them.

Seemore Says

Most insects are harmless to humans, but some of them can really bug you. Flies can spread disease by infecting food on eating implements. Keep your food fly-free!

Your teeth

Your teeth are covered with a layer of protective enamel made from hard, crystallized calcium. This enamel layer makes your teeth tough enough to withstand a lifetime of hard wear and tear – but only if you look after them properly. Although it is the toughest substance in the body, enamel is also vulnerable to decay.

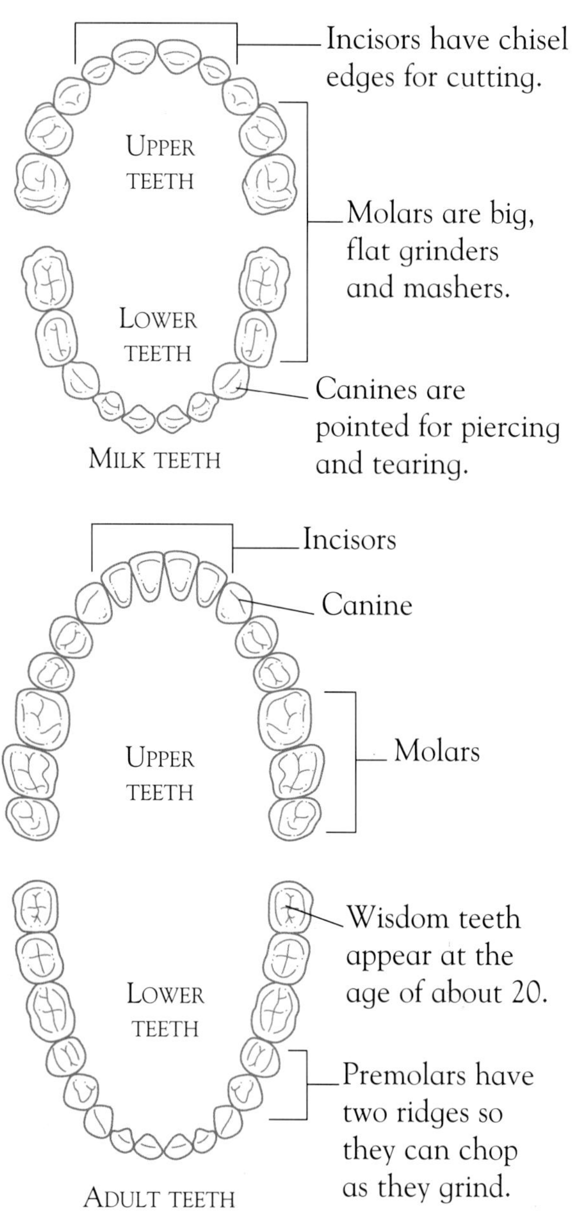
Incisors have chisel edges for cutting.
UPPER TEETH
Molars are big, flat grinders and mashers.
LOWER TEETH
Canines are pointed for piercing and tearing.
MILK TEETH
Incisors
Canine
UPPER TEETH
Molars
LOWER TEETH
Wisdom teeth appear at the age of about 20.
Premolars have two ridges so they can chop as they grind.
ADULT TEETH

What teeth are for

Humans are omnivores, which means we can eat just about any plant or animal. Your first set of 20 milk teeth will be replaced and, by the time you reach your 20s, you will have a full set of 32 adult teeth. Adult teeth have several different shapes to help us rip, tear, crush, and grind different foods.

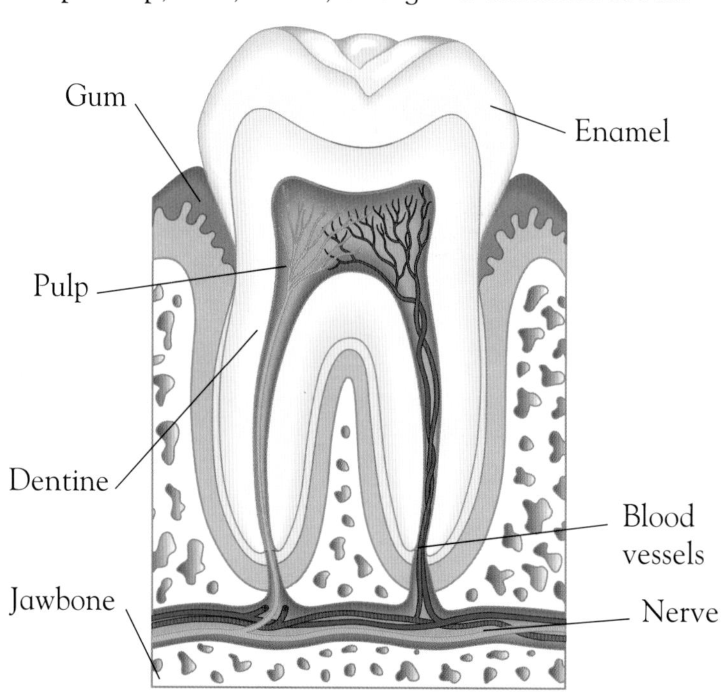
Gum
Enamel
Pulp
Dentine
Blood vessels
Jawbone
Nerve

Teeth are alive

The part of the tooth you can see is made of hard white enamel. Beneath that is bone like tissue called dentine. At the center of every tooth is soft pulp in which blood vessels and nerves are located.

Tooth decay

Plaque is a mixture of food remnants and bacteria that builds up on your teeth every day. The bacteria produce an acid that eats through enamel.

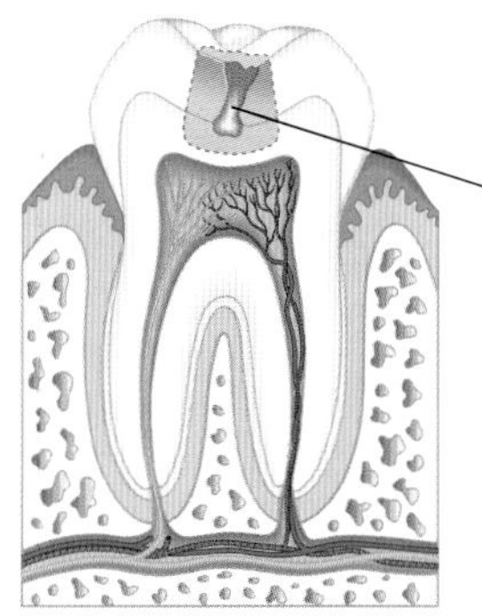

Decay has gone through the enamel to the dentine.

DECAYED TOOTH

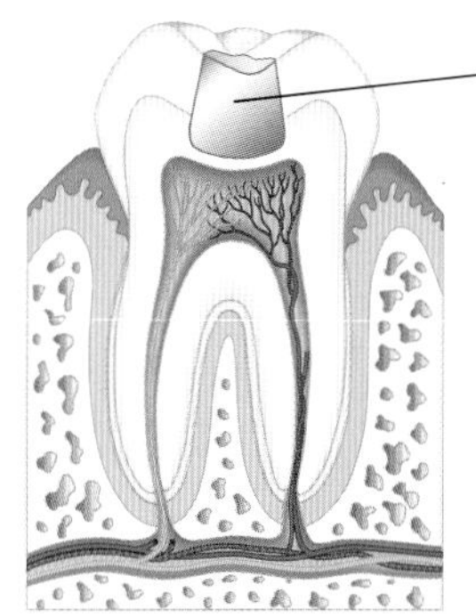

The dentist drills away the decay and fills the tooth with a mixture of metals. This prevents further decay.

TOOTH WITH A FILLING

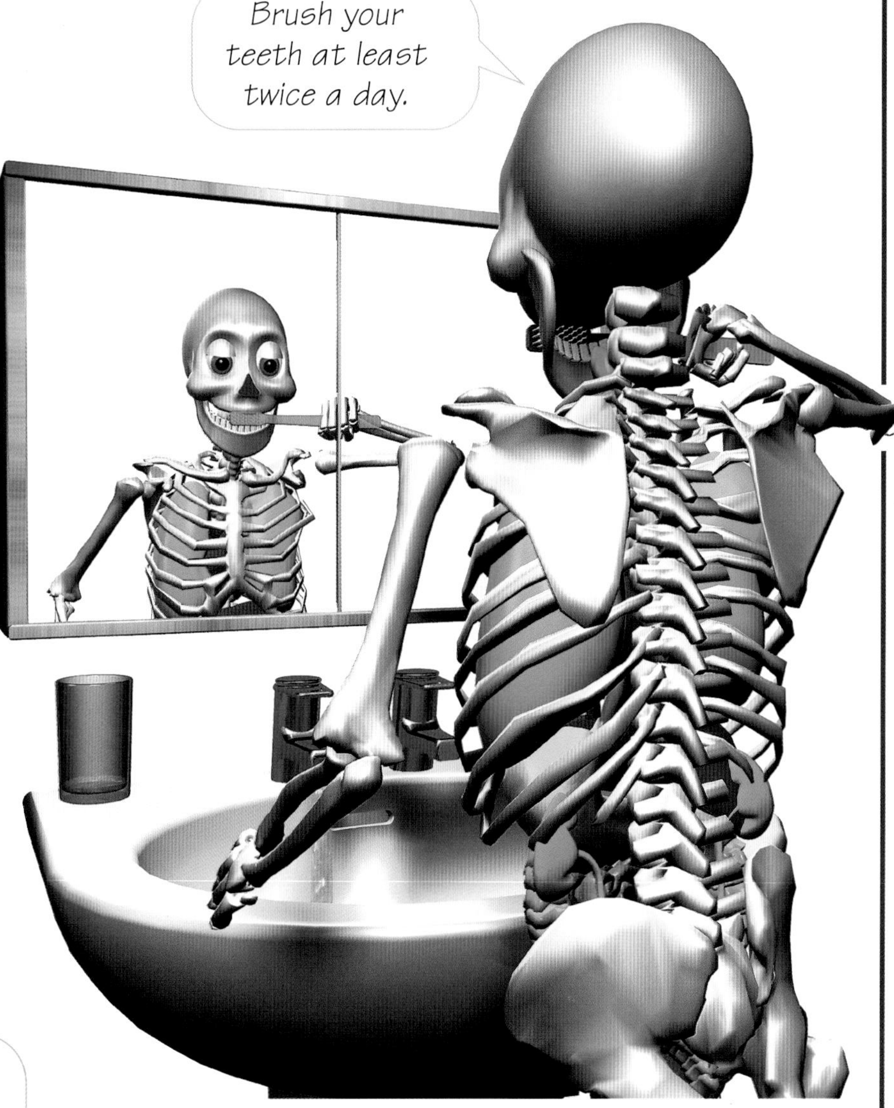

Brush your teeth at least twice a day.

Badly decayed teeth have to be pulled out!

All about teeth

Seemore Says

Some people wear braces to push their teeth into a straight and even position. They may need to have one or more teeth removed to prevent overcrowding when the straightened teeth move back into line.

Risky business

Everything we do involves some sort of risk – even crossing the road or riding a bike. We all want to have as much fun and to live as long as possible, so we should choose our risks carefully and steer clear of the real killers. Some risky activities – such as sunbathing, smoking, and drinking too much alcohol – can be easily avoided.

Made in the shade

It is well known that people who get badly sunburned as children are more likely to develop skin cancer when they're older. There are several precautions you can take to protect your skin while you have fun in the Sun.

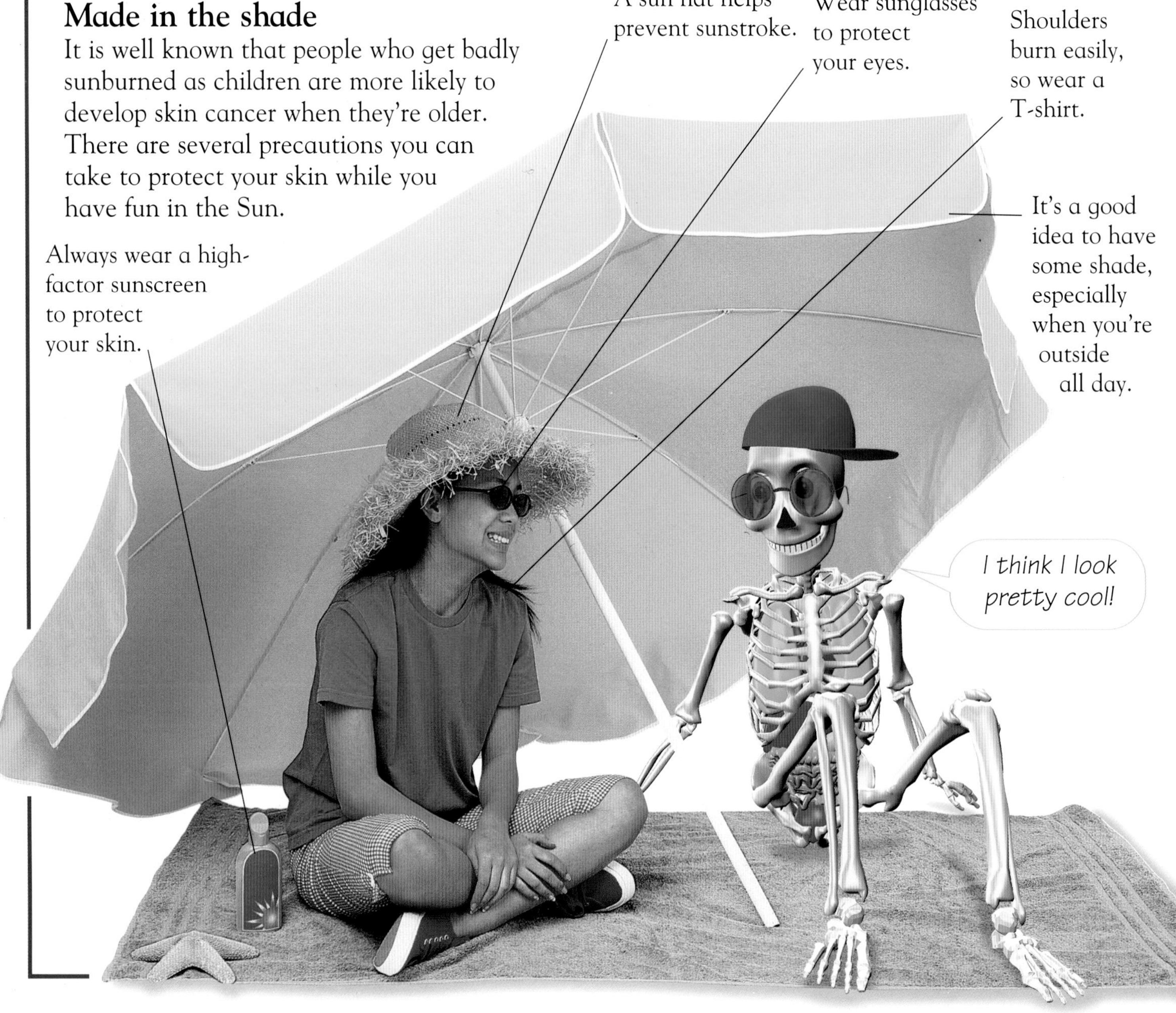

A sun hat helps prevent sunstroke.
Wear sunglasses to protect your eyes.
Shoulders burn easily, so wear a T-shirt.
It's a good idea to have some shade, especially when you're outside all day.
Always wear a high-factor sunscreen to protect your skin.
I think I look pretty cool!

Seemore Says

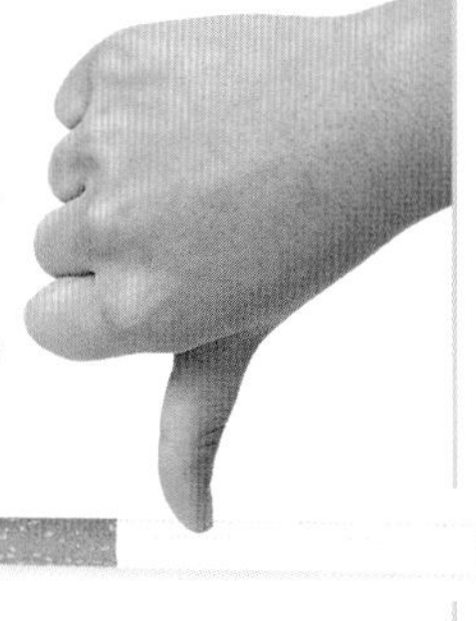

The biggest health risk that brings the smallest amount of pleasure is smoking. 90% of smokers start before the age of 18 and it takes as little as four weeks to become addicted to nicotine. Long-term smokers often develop serious illnesses and many die early.

Other bad ideas

The runners-up for Seemore's award for bad ideas and unnecessary risks are:

1. Diving headfirst into water if the depth is unknown.
2. Playing near electrified rails or electricity substations.
3. Running into the road from behind parked vehicles or near a curve.
4. Cutting toward yourself when using a knife.
5. Putting a radio or any other electrical device near your bath or shower.
6. Running while holding scissors.

Can you think of any more?

Alcohol limit

Too much beer, wine, or liquor makes people drunk. As well as damaging health, alcohol affects judgement. Anyone who drives a car after they've been drinking risks other people's lives as well as their own (*see page 41*).

Keep your hat on

A fall from a bike or skates can be a brain-scrambling experience. Besides protecting against broken bones, a helmet can stop a bad blow to your head from causing brain damage. A bruised brain can malfunction and may even change your personality.

Skin color

Medical help

There is more to staying healthy than eating well and keeping fit: sometimes you need the help of the professionals. If any condition is worrying you or won't go away on its own, ask your doctor about it. There are hundreds of kinds of treatments they can either give or recommend. If the problem is really urgent, your family doctor will help get you checked into a hospital.

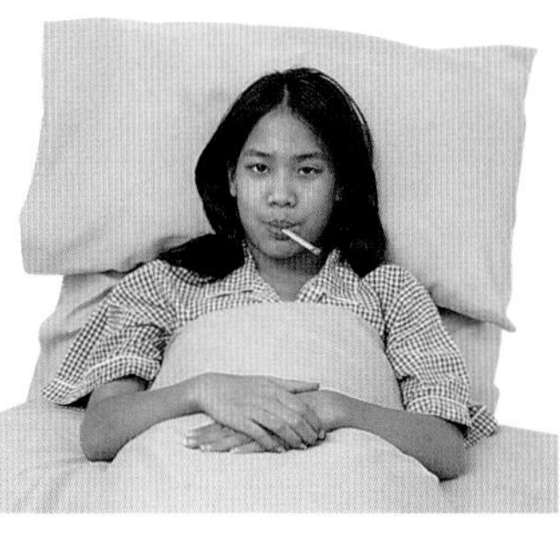

1 Stomach pain
Beth wakes up with sharp pains in her right side and a high temperature.

2 Doctor, doctor
Beth's mother thinks it might be serious, so she calls the doctor. Because the problem is urgent, the receptionist at the surgery arranges an appointment for Beth with the doctor that morning.

Beth tells the doctor what's wrong.

The doctor asks her some questions.

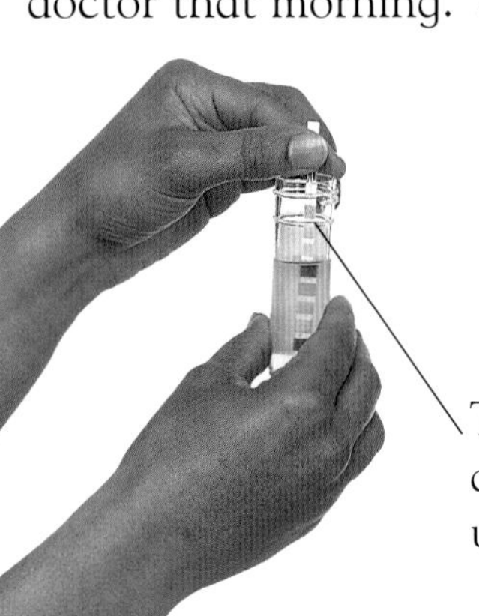

The doctor asks for a urine sample.

3 Urine test
The urine is tested for infection, diabetes, kidney problems, and any signs of blood. The results are negative, so the doctor thinks the pains may be caused by Beth's appendix. She needs to go to hospital for an operation.

Beth breathes through a tube.

4 Out for the count
Just before the operation, the anesthetist gives Beth a drug that sends her into a deep sleep so that she won't feel anything during the operation.

5 Removing the appendix

Once Beth is safely asleep, the surgeon can begin the operation. He makes a cut in her right side and removes the infected appendix. Then he stitches up the wound.

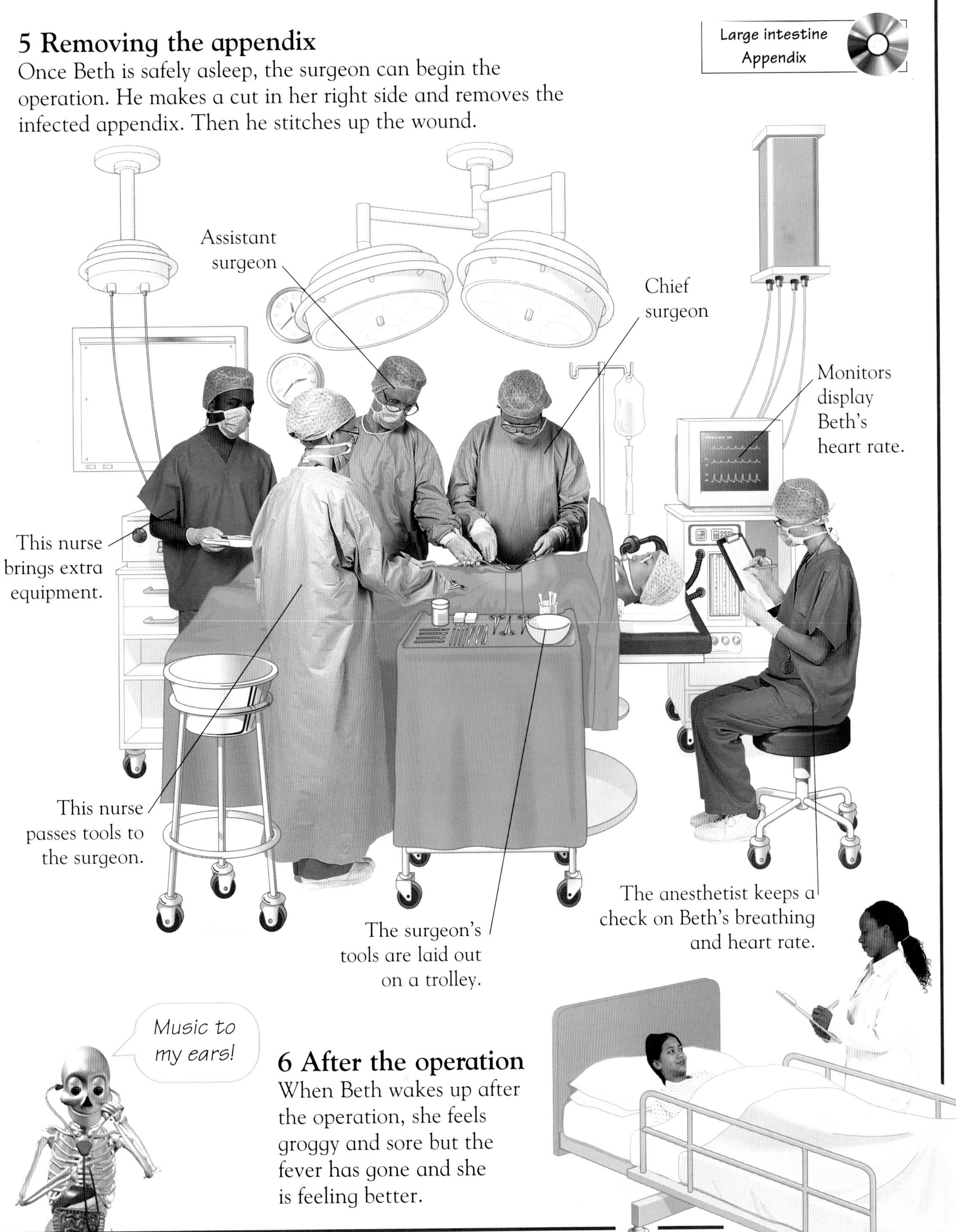

Large intestine
Appendix
Assistant surgeon
Chief surgeon
Monitors display Beth's heart rate.
This nurse brings extra equipment.
This nurse passes tools to the surgeon.
The surgeon's tools are laid out on a trolley.
The anesthetist keeps a check on Beth's breathing and heart rate.
Music to my ears!

6 After the operation

When Beth wakes up after the operation, she feels groggy and sore but the fever has gone and she is feeling better.

First aid

Accidents happen, so you need to be prepared for them. The first rule for dealing with any injury is "THINK!". If the accident is a minor cut, sprain, or burn, there are a few common-sense techniques to help you minimize pain and damage. If you are ever at the scene of a more serious accident, stay calm so you can call for help.

Hands off!

Electricity is a killer. If someone is electrocuted and is still touching the live wire, anyone who touches them will be electrocuted as well. Call for help immediately.

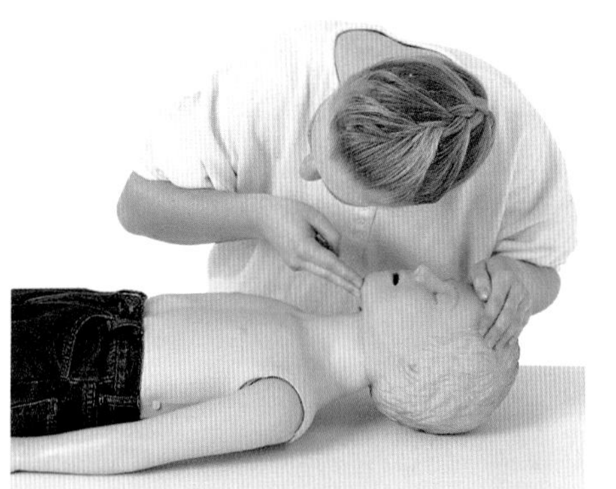

First-aid courses

A first-aid course will teach you how to perform life saving techniques such as mouth-to-mouth resuscitation, and how to take care of people who have been injured. Ask your parents or your teacher, or phone the local branch of the Red Cross to find out if there's a course suitable for you.

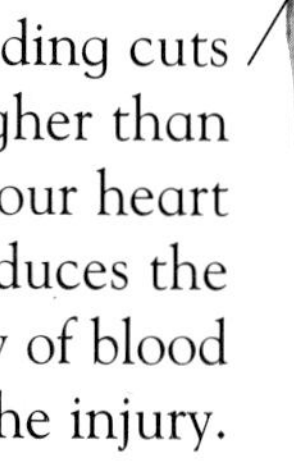

Holding cuts higher than your heart reduces the flow of blood to the injury.

Treating burns

Minor burns should be plunged into cold water immediately. This eases the pain and helps to slow further damage to the skin through exposure to oxygen.

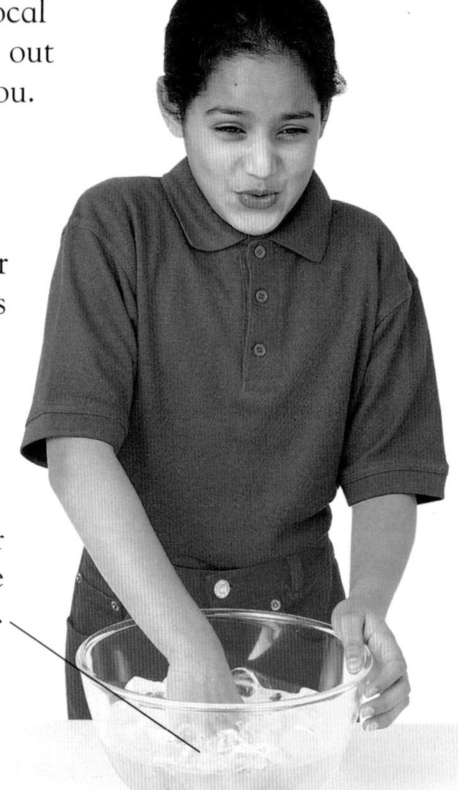

Cold water reduces the pain of a burn.

Treating cuts

Hold a cut higher than your heart to slow the flow of blood. This gives the blood a better chance to form clots. Applying pressure also slows blood flow.

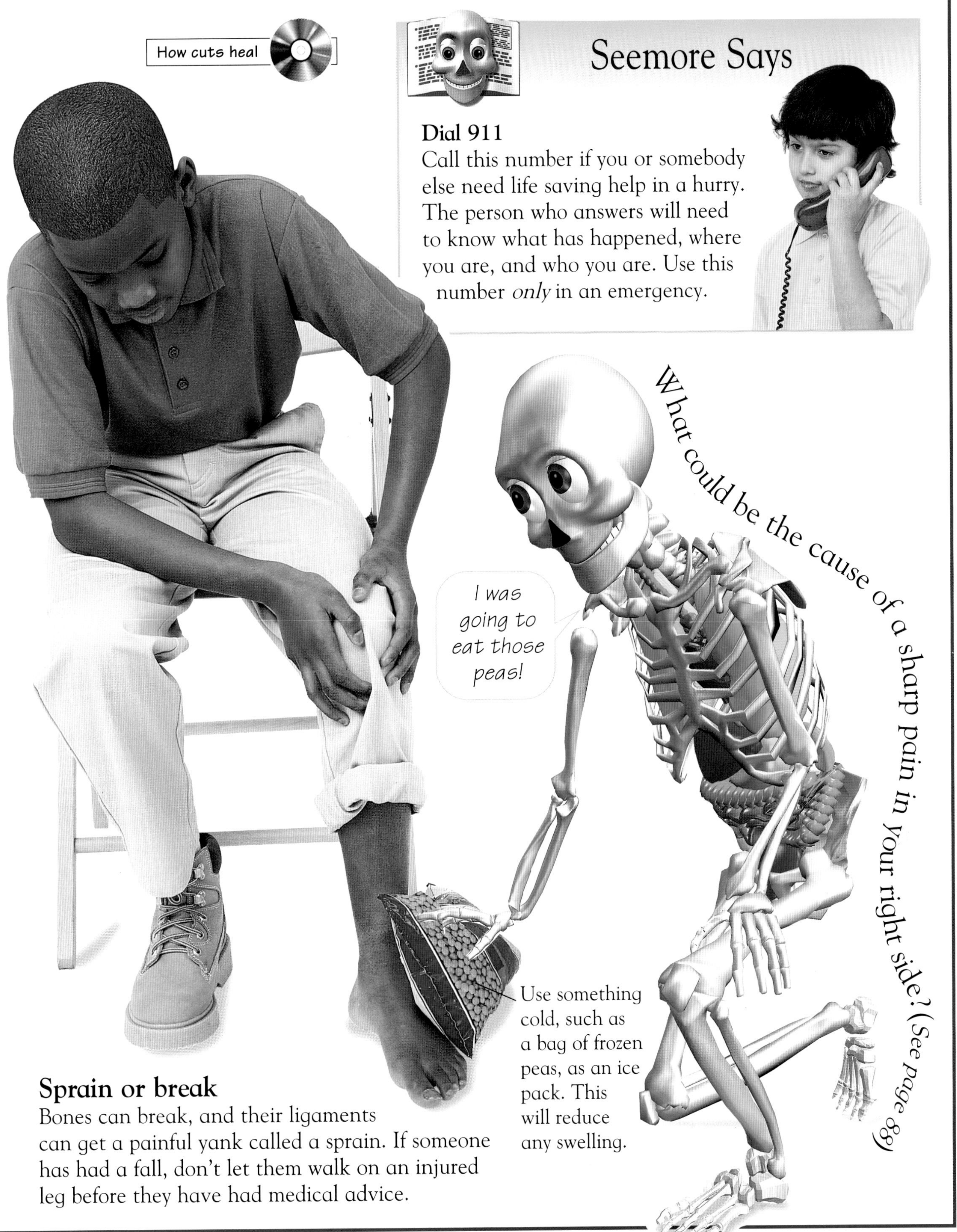

How cuts heal
I was going to eat those peas!
What could be the cause of a sharp pain in your right side? (See page 88)

Seemore Says

Dial 911
Call this number if you or somebody else need life saving help in a hurry. The person who answers will need to know what has happened, where you are, and who you are. Use this number *only* in an emergency.

Use something cold, such as a bag of frozen peas, as an ice pack. This will reduce any swelling.

Sprain or break
Bones can break, and their ligaments can get a painful yank called a sprain. If someone has had a fall, don't let them walk on an injured leg before they have had medical advice.

Ultimate human body

What is the ultimate human body? Everyone has a different answer to this question, depending on what they value most. Some people idolize great athletes or admire those who have overcome great adversity. Others think that the way they look is more important than how they feel. What would your ultimate human body be like?

Extra brain room.

Some recovery!
In 1999, Lance Armstrong won the 1,400 mile (2,300 km) Tour de France bike race by a solid eight minutes. This achievement is all the more incredible because, just two years earlier, he was being treated for an extreme form of cancer.

Way to go!
If you have a disability, you may have to work your body harder than others. Visually impaired people develop their sense of touch to read the raised letters of Braille.

Blind people use their fingertips to read Braille.

Spare leg for use when the others get tired.

Future bodies

Scientists are learning how to alter plants and animals genetically. Already, they can take genes from one animal and splice them into the chromosomes of another. If you could make any changes you like to the human body, what would you do?

Under the knife

Some people go to extreme measures to make their bodies look the way they want them to. This might involve spending several hours in the gym every day, or even having plastic surgery to change particular features.

I could be a movie star!

Will humans fly one day?

What is the ultimate human body?

After weighing up all the evidence, Seemore has made his choice. Here are a few clues:

- It's got fantastic systems that work together.
- It's unlike any other body that has ever been.
- It's built from the finest material known to last a lifetime.

Have you guessed yet?

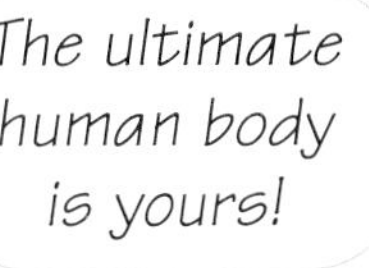

The ultimate human body is yours!

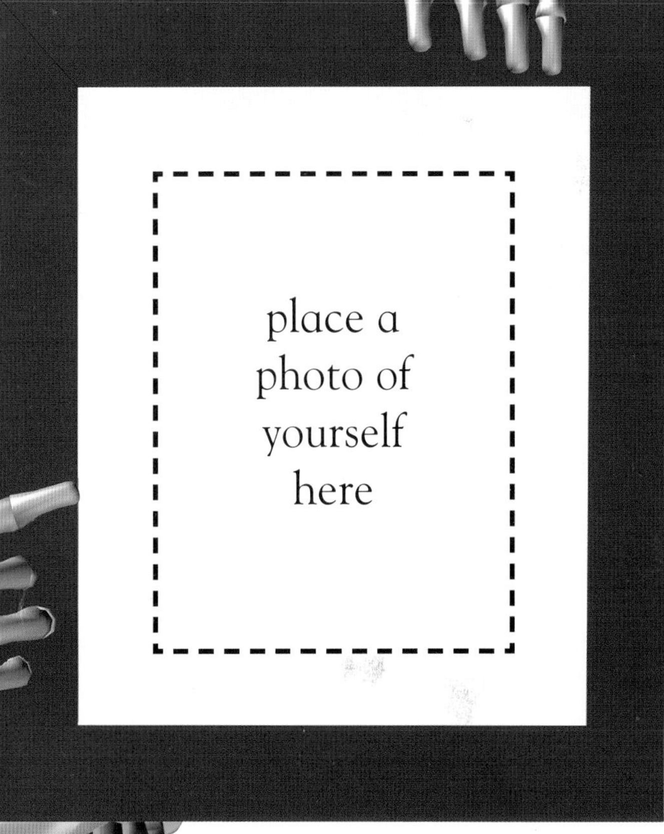

Index

Acknowledgments

The author would like to thank Bill Schaser – an inspiring teacher.

Dorling Kindersley would like to thank Dawn Rowley for editorial assistance.

Studio Cactus would like to thank Chris Bernstein for compiling the index, Polly Boyd and Fiona Wild for proofreading, Emily Hedges for picture research, Susan St. Louis for her help with starting up the project, and Laura Watson for design assistance. Thanks also to Melanie Brown for the loan of her hats and to Calvin and Ethan D'Andrea for their original drawings. A special thank you to Louise Dick at Dorling Kindersley for her invaluable help with sourcing illustrations.

Photography
Children (Safi Dewshi, Aimée Ford-King, Gemma Loke, Mishali Patel, Joe Wood, Daniel Williams) photographed by Andy Crawford.

Dorling Kindersley would like to thank the following for their kind permission to reproduce their photographs: (t=top, c=center, r=right, l=left)

Actionplus/Y.Vuillaume: 92 cl; Educational and Scientific Products Ltd UK c/o Denoyer-Geppert: 11c; Mary Evans Picture Library: 53 tr; Mattel UK Ltd: 52 bl; NASA: 68 tr; 80 tl; Rex Features London: 53 c; 58; Science Photo Library: Alex Bartel, 71 cl; Biophoto Associates (muscle cells), 32 cr; John Durham (bone cells), 32 c; Lowell Georgia, 42 br; Dr Kari Lounatmaa, 83 cl; Peter Menzel, 17 br; Prof. P. Motta/Dept. of Anatomy/ University "La Sapienza," Rome, 20tr; National Cancer Institute (blood cells), 32 cl; Dr Yorgas Nikas, 54 bl; Quest, 13 cr; Professor John Sloane, University of Liverpool: 35 tr; Tony Stone: John Riley (right grandparents, parents, child), 52; David Young Wolff (left grandparents), 52; The Water Monopoly: 71 b.

Illustrations
Alternative View Studios (www.avstudios.com) Seemore 3D modeling and digital artwork; Peter Bull Art Studios: 16-17 c, 17 bl, 18-19 r, 23 cl, 30-31 tc, 36 r, 48 b.

Human Body Explorer CD-ROM

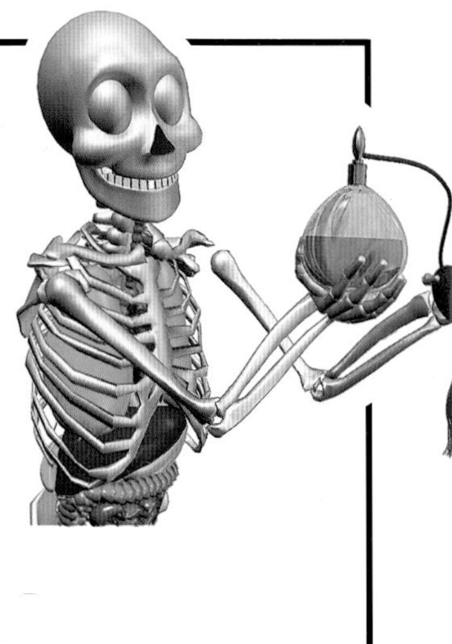

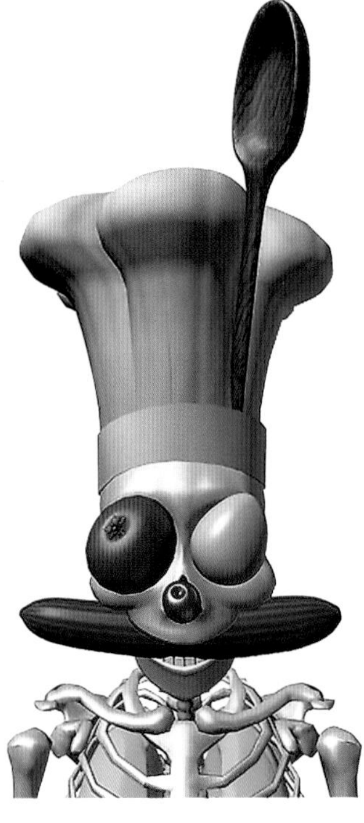

Build me a body Stomach/intestines
Digestive system What am I made of?

This box appears throughout this book to indicate links between the content of the book and the ***Human Body Explorer*** CD-ROM. Seemore Skinless guides the user through the CD-ROM'S four fun activity areas – *Build me a body*, *My day*, *Take me apart*, and *What am I made of?* Your child can learn more about the body as he or she plays with Seemore and answers his body quiz questions. The CD-ROM also features an alphabetical search facility that enables your child to access information on any human body topic at the click of a mouse.

The CD-ROM complements the material provided in this book although both the CD-ROM and the book have been designed to be used independently of each other.

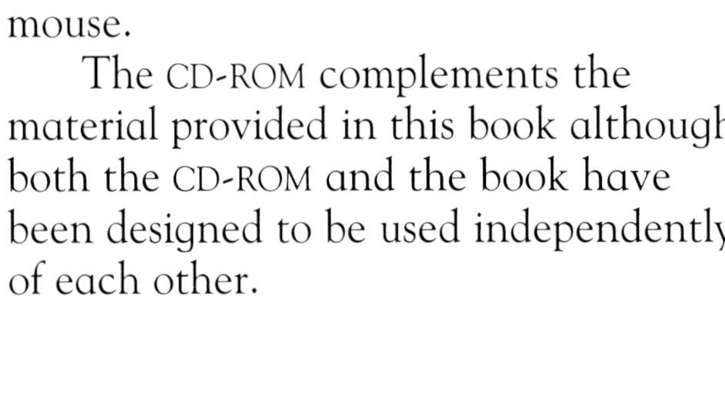

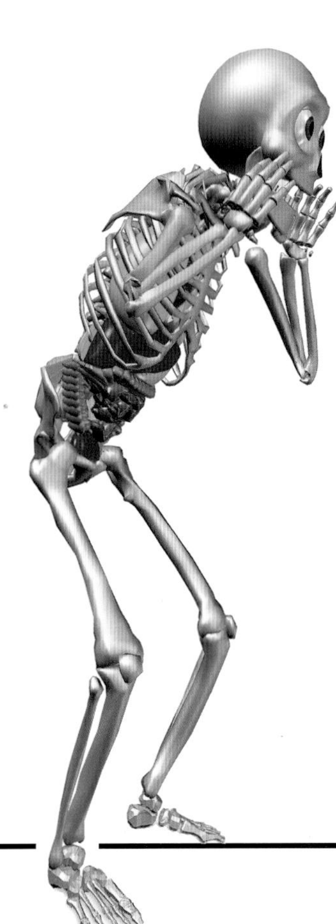

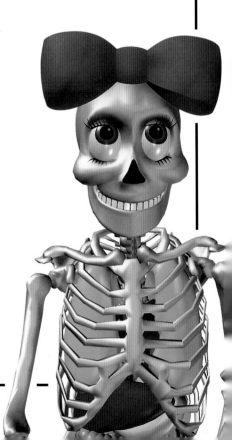